THE LAKE ERIE SHORE

RON BROWN

THE LAKE ERIE SHORE

Ontario's Forgotten South Coast

NATURAL HERITAGE BOOKS
A MEMBER OF THE DUNDURN GROUP
TORONTO

Copy-edited by Shannon Whibbs
Designed by Erin Mallory
Printed and bound in Canada by Transcontinental

Library and Archives Canada Cataloguing in Publication

Brown, Ron, 1945–
   The Lake Erie shore : Ontario's forgotten south coast / by Ron Brown.

Includes bibliographical references and index.
ISBN 978-1-55488-388-2

   1. Erie, Lake, Region--History. I. Title.

FC3095.L335B76 2009   971.3'3   C2009-900102-0

1 2 3 4 5   13 12 11 10 09

Conseil des Arts du Canada   Canada Council for the Arts   Canadä   ONTARIO ARTS COUNCIL CONSEIL DES ARTS DE L'ONTARIO

We acknowledge the support of the **Canada Council for the Arts** and the **Ontario Arts Council** for our publishing program. We also acknowledge the financial support of the **Government of Canada** through the **Book Publishing Industry Development Program** and **The Association for the Export of Canadian Books**, and the **Government of Ontario** through the **Ontario Book Publishers Tax Credit** program, and the **Ontario Media Development Corporation**.

Care has been taken to trace the ownership of copyright material used in this book. The author and the publisher welcome any information enabling them to rectify any references or credits in subsequent editions.
                                                                    J. Kirk Howard, President

www.dundurn.com
Published by Natural Heritage Books
A Member of The Dundurn Group

Front cover photo: Port Dover. Photo by Ron Brown
Back cover photo: Fort Erie. Photo by Ron Brown
Unless otherwise indicated, all images are credited to the author

Dundurn Press	Gazelle Book Services Limited	Dundurn Press
3 Church Street, Suite 500	White Cross Mills	2250 Military Road
Toronto, Ontario, Canada	High Town, Lancaster, England	Tonawanda, NY
M5E 1M2	LA1 4XS	U.S.A. 14150

CONTENTS

ACKNOWLEDGEMENTS

No book on local history or heritage could work without the hard work and participation of local heritage enthusiasts. In general, I want to acknowledge the libraries in Leamington and Fort Erie, and the Port Dover Harbour Museum for housing a wonderful store of local material, and for making it available for this book.

A number of individuals went out of their way to provide information and help with travel to this forgotten area. These include Robert Honor, owner of Honor's Bed and Breakfast in Amherstburg, and coordinator of heritage walks in that historic town; Clark Hoskin, manager of Tourism and Economic Development for Norfolk County; John Cooper of the Lake Erie Management Unit in the Ontario Ministry of Natural Resources office in London; Sandra Bradt, director of tourism for the Convention and Visitors Bureau of Windsor, Essex County, and Pelee Island; Karen Cummings, co-ordinator of Tourism, Development and Marketing for the County of Elgin; Stephen Francom, manager and curator of the Elgin County Archives; and Caralee Grummett of the Fort Erie Economic Development and Tourism Corporation in Fort Erie.

The many local histories and collections in our libraries make the region come alive and provide the small stories as well as the big picture. In this digital age, the Internet is now full of individual contributions to the lore of the local area. These books, articles, and websites are listed at the conclusion of the book. They are a true reflection of an enthusiasm for the heritage of the places of the Lake Erie. For all these individuals Lake Erie is not forgotten.

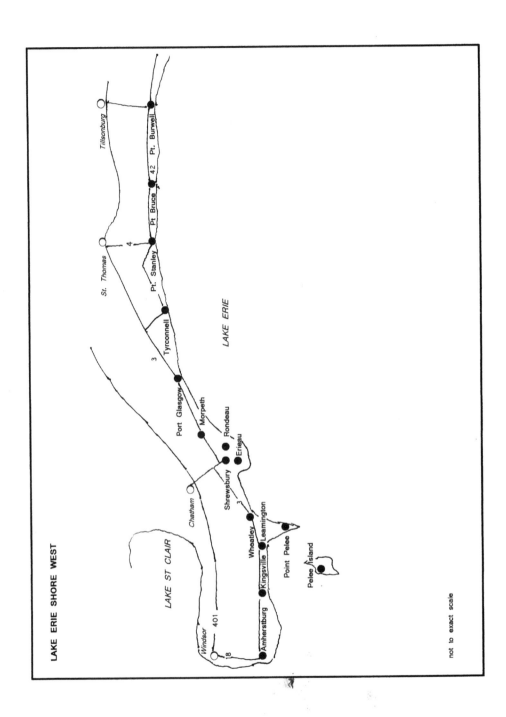

LAKE ERIE SHORE WEST

LAKE ST CLAIR

Windsor

401

8

Amherstburg

Kingsville

Leamington

Wheatley

Point Pelee

Pelee Island

Chatham

3

Shrewsbury

Erieau

Rondeau

Morpeth

Port Glasgow

3

Tyrconnell

LAKE ERIE

Pt. Stanley

4

St. Thomas

Pt. Bruce

42

Pt. Burwell

Tillsonburg

not to exact scale

LAKE ERIE SHORE EAST

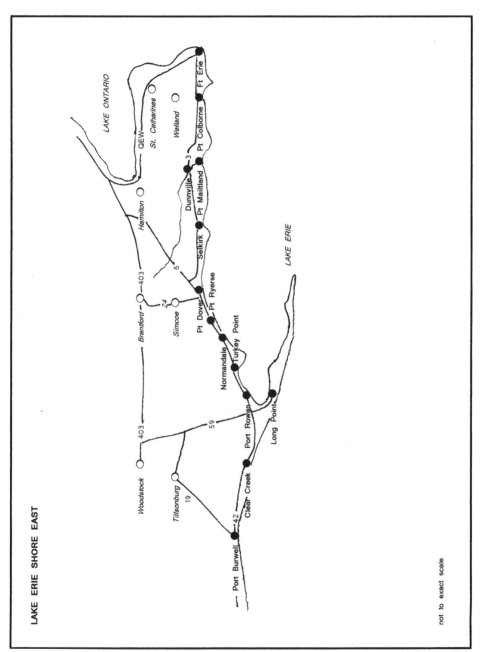

not to exact scale

INTRODUCTION

Ontario's Forgotten South Coast

W hen you think about it, what exactly is it that makes the Canadian shore of Lake Erie so special? It's not its physical features, for it lacks the soaring cliffs of the Bruce Peninsula, the white mountains of Lake Huron, or the giant red outcrops of Superior's magnificent coastline. Nor is there anything like the smooth, sculpted pink shoals that line the Thirty Thousand Islands of Georgian Bay. Rather, it offers a rather dreary coast consisting of a monotonous cliff line punctuated by marshes and long sandy spits that jut far into the lake.

It's not its developments, for the towns and villages that line it are small and often little-changed over their existence. No CN Towers here, no "Distillery Districts," Ontario Places, or Gardiner Expressways.

What makes it special are in fact exactly those things — the absence of the grand. Rather, it is a place to explore the past, the ecology, the places — all of which are little known outside of its own sphere.

Here you find the northern reaches of the lush Carolinian forests, plants found nowhere else in Ontario. Here too is one of Ontario's only three UNESCO World Biosphere Reserves, as well as cactuses, tall grass prairies, and one of Canada's Heritage rivers. The waters of the lake are among Ontario's most dangerous, their shallow depths littered with hundreds of doomed ships. It is a lake of unpredictable tidal waves and, some say, its own "monster."

Its shores harbour a string of active fishing ports, home to the world's largest freshwater fishing fleet, and indeed the last fishing fleet on the Great Lakes. Picturesque harbours contain fish stores, net sheds, and historic light houses, and in one case, a castle. In other cases, the Erie shore can be a "ghost coast." Where schooners once set sail with barley or lumber, only rotten cribbing lies, hotels and stores sit empty, mill sites have only their overgrown ponds to tell of busy milling days.

Then there is its human history — fugitive slaves escaping their humiliating servitude, heroines rescuing the crew of a sinking ship, a "witch" doctor, an imperious "emperor" after whom many a place has been named, nefarious rum-runners, and the mysterious, little-known pre-historic inhabitants.

Yet for those who know Erie's shores, and love them, they are anything but forgotten. But for those who live in Ontario's sprawling metropoli, or are more used to the traditional cottage country, Erie's shores are little known. For most of Ontario, Lake Erie is indeed Ontario's forgotten south coast.

PART ONE

❧

The Story of a Lake

THE MAKING OF A LAKE

Tidal Waves, Monsters, and Dead Zones

C ompared to the millions of millennia that water has existed on Earth, Lake Erie is but a mere newcomer. Its current form is less than 4,000 years old. Nor will it remain thus for much longer.

Lake Erie is a product of the last ice age. For thousands of years, massive glaciers covered most of eastern Canada, and parts of the northeastern United States, an ice sheet that some scientists estimate may have been more than three kilometres thick in some places. What the land looked like before this big freeze is anybody's guess. What is known is that the basins occupied by today's Great Lakes likely existed in some form, and were deepened by the enormous scouring of the advancing ice sheets.

But some 20,000 years ago, when the earth began to warm again, and the ice began to melt, the glaciers did not recede in a uniform way. Rather, the mass broke into irregular lobes, one forming to the east of today's lake, another to the north. As the ice melted, a lake formed, which scientists have named Lake Maumee.[1] While its elevation varied during the melt, its waters flowed westward through today's Michigan, and then down the Mississippi.

But the great glaciers weren't done yet. A cold snap enlarged them once more, creating yet a different lake, one which was named Lake Whittlesey, but whose waters again flowed west through Michigan. Then the glaciers retreated once more and exposed a startlingly different outlet for the lake waters, through an earlier version of today's Niagara Gorge. Then, when the ice sheets advanced yet again, and filled the gorge with glacial debris, that outlet became blocked and the waters were forced eastward through today's Mohawk Valley in New York State.

Finally, the ice began to recede for good. As it did, the Niagara Gorge again became Lake Erie's outlet. Because the original gorge was now filled with debris, the waters carved out a new channel. That channel is marked by today's Niagara Gorge, where it begins its sharp bend at the famous whirlpool. The old gorge, now buried, lies between the whirlpool and the community of St. David's.

But because the enormous weight of the ice continued to depress the land, that outlet was about fifty metres lower than it is today, and so too were the waters of Lake Erie. That lower elevation meant that much of the lake's western section stood high and dry, an area that today lies west of Long Point. The islands of the western lake, Pelee Island, Middle Island, and the American islands formed a land bridge, allowing the passage of animals and some of the earliest human inhabitants.

Finally, about 4,000 years ago, with the ice far to the north, its weight gone, the land around the Niagara Gorge began to rise, allowing the lake to fill to almost its present levels.

But how much longer will it survive as a lake? As the great falls of the Niagara River continue to erode their way upstream, they will eventually reach Lake Erie itself, where as they erode farther into the lake bed, will lower the lake and turn it into a massive river.

The Shape of the Lake

Despite being one the smallest of the "Great" Lakes, Erie, at nearly 26,000 square kilometres, remains the tenth largest in the world. Among the Great Lakes, however, only Ontario is smaller by volume. Nearly 390 kilometres long, the lake at its widest is ninety-two kilometres. It is however, the shallowest of the lakes with an average depth of only nineteen metres. While its deepest points, east of Long Point, plunge to sixty-four metres, its western waters go down a mere thirteen metres. Still, it remains the only one of the lakes whose lowest point is actually above sea level.

With only a handful of rivers flowing into it, Erie's waters are provided mainly by the Detroit River. The Niagara River remains its sole outlet. Because of its shallowness, the waters of the lake renew themselves completely once every two-and-a-half years.[2]

Rock Point Provincial Park offers fossil displays in its shoreline bedrock.

Of its total shoreline length of nearly 1,400 kilometres, slightly less than half lies in Ontario, the remainder laps the shores of the American states of Michigan, Ohio, Pennsylvania, and New York. Those states contain no fewer than three counties which bear the name "Erie," while none of the six counties or regions on the Ontario side carry the name of the lake on which they lie.

Unlike the rocky Ontario northlands, Lake Erie's physical shoreline characteristics have resulted directly from the forces of the last ice age, although moderated somewhat by wind and water. The eastern section of the shore is a level and poorly drained clay plain with few shoreline features. Beaches and sand dunes alternate with flat, rocky headlands, the latter often exhibiting spectacular fossil displays (Rock Point Provincial Park is one of the best sites from which to observe them). A flat, limestone shoreline surrounds the elusive Point Abino lighthouse. Inland lie extensive areas of peat bogs.

Port Colborne marks the entrance to the busy and historic Welland Canal, completed in 1927. Immediately to the west of the harbour looms a soaring dune locally named the Sugarloaf, a feature which still serves as a navigation aid for vessels plying the lake.

The only significant break in the shoreline comes at Port Maitland where the wide, sluggish waters of the Grand River seep into the lake. A heritage waterway, the Grand begins its run in a wide swamp north of Dundalk in a wide swamp known as the Osprey Wetlands. As it winds its way southward through cattle country it gradually picks up tributaries until, at Grand Valley, it begins to resemble a river. At Fergus it begins to tumble through the fairyland rockscapes of the Elora Gorge, where hole-in-wall and dry waterfalls rock formations have created an almost otherworldly waterscape. Beyond the gorge, it has carved out a wide, meandering valley where the water power gave rise to a string of mill towns with names like Conestoga, Galt, Glen Morris, Paris, Brantford, Caledonia, and Dunnville, which is situated at the mouth of the river. The river is wide, its banks marshy and home to a variety of wildlife species.

West of the Grand, the shoreline continues to be low and occasionally rocky, interrupted only by a few small creeks, such as Stoney Creek, which provided mill sites for the community of Selkirk, and Nanticoke Creek, which performed the same role for the village of Nanticoke. In the latter community the cove created by the creek's entrance into the lake was large enough to spawn a small harbour.

Finally, west of Nanticoke, the typical cliffs of Lake Erie begin to appear, inspiring the appropriately named Port Dover, named after the famed cliffs in England. Here, the confluence of the Lynn River and Black Creek have cut through the cliffs, creating water power for mills and allowing a deep and protected harbour for schooners and fishing boats. It is here that the shoreline enters a region known as the Norfolk Sand Plain. This historic area is the result of an extensive delta laid down when the waters of the melting ice sheets poured into the waters of a higher Lake Whittlesey. Here, the cliffs of sand and clay reach heights of twenty-five to thirty metres. Along the way, creeks have carved deep valleys and spawned little ports such as Normandale and Fishers Glen.

One of the highest points overlooks Turkey Point, a promontory that briefly proved useful for a military role. Inland, the sandy soils attracted a community of farmers, grateful for the stone free and tillable soils. However, the sands quickly lost their fertility and by 1900 were largely abandoned. Winds turned extensive stretches of farmland into a blowing sand desert. Reforestation halted much of the erosion until it was discovered, in the early 1920s, that these conditions were ideal for tobacco and the region soon became Ontario's most productive tobacco belt.

The next stretch of shoreline contains one of the lake's most prominent natural features, Long Point, and is now a UNESCO World Biosphere Reserve. The reserve boundary incorporates both the long spit and Turkey Point, as well. The two points of land nearly encircle a shallow bay, with the latter spit extending to the southwest and the former to the southeast.

The point, which juts thirty kilometres into the lake, contains the most extensive and varied collection of ecosystems among the entire Great Lakes shorelines. Ever shifting, it continues to be formed by sands and silts swept easterly by the lake's currents. The Turkey Point section, however, owes its orientation to currents circling from the east. Beyond the intense development of cottages near the neck of Long Point, the protected section harbours more than 270 species of birds and 700 plant species, 90 of which are classified as rare. Shallow bays, sandbars, dunes, scrublands, ponds, and marshes are all found along the extensive spit.

Designated in 1986 as a UNESCO World Biosphere Reserve, it is one of only three in Ontario and one of six in all of Canada. With most of it now under the ownership of the Canadian Wildlife Foundation, the reserve consists of the core protected zone, and a wider buffer zone that extends into the lake as well as along the shoreline.

As Lake Erie's shoreline continues west from Long Point, the bluffs resume once more. But among them lies one striking anomaly, the Houghton Sand

The Turkey Point marshes contain a vital ecosystem and form part of the Long Point UNESCO World Biosphere Reserve.

Hills. Unlike the uniformity of the cliffs to this point, silt and sand, the sand hills are nothing but sand. It has earned its local nickname, Ontario's "biggest sand pile." For a stretch of about two kilometres, these mounds of pure sand loom nearly one hundred metres above the lake. As with much of the Erie shore, the sand pile traces its origins to the massive stream of meltwater which poured from the glaciers into the higher waters of Lake Whittlesey.

Again, the bluffs lower until they reach yet another of the Erie spits, Point aux Pins. This 1,800-hectare peninsula of early Carolinian forests curves eight kilometres into the lake enclosing a large, shallow bay known as Rondeau Bay.

The stretch of shoreline between these two points is also notable for the lack of rivers or major creeks that flow into the lake. A series of beach ridges and remnants of Lake Whittlesey force most drainage northward into the Thames River watershed, which parallels the Erie shoreline in this area.

The next Erie spit is probably the lake's most famous, better known than even Long Point. That is Point Pelee. It is known especially for being the most

southerly point of mainland Canada, with a latitude more southerly than northern California. It is known too, even among non-naturalists, as being one of the most spectacular gathering places for the monarch butterfly as they annually migrate to the mountains of central Mexico.

At ten kilometres long, it extends almost straight into the lake, formed by currents that attack it from both east and west. Beaches line both sides, culminating in a pencil point of sand that stabs into the lake before narrowing and slipping beneath the waves. The length

The Houghton Sand Hills were once a massive sand delta when Lake Erie's water levels were much higher.

of this spit can vary from year to year. It can stretch two kilometres from the edge of the forest, or it can disappear entirely as it did in 2007, following a particularly stormy spring.

Its natural makeup is outstanding. It contains dense Carolinian forests of silver maple, black walnut, red cedar tulip, and honey locust trees, many of them wrapped in vines of Virginia creeper and poison ivy. Open savannahs display rare grasses and cactuses. An enclosed marsh is covered with water lilies, bulrushes, and the hop tree, a member of the citrus family, which can be found even as far south as Mexico. While the once numerous bear and deer population is much reduced (the bears are gone), the animal population contains several species of frogs and turtles, snakes and bats, and the reintroduced southern flying squirrel, which weigh in at little more than seventy-five grams.

Although Point Pelee counts as the most southerly point of mainland Canada, Canada's actual southernmost shores lie farther out in the lake. Pelee Island is visible from Point Pelee only as a pencil-thin line on the watery horizon. Once part of a land bridge connecting the north and south shores of the lake, Pelee

The shifting sands of Point Pelee reflect the currents of Lake Erie.

Because of Lake Erie's vicious easterly winds, Pelee Island's lakeside homes use stilts to protect them from the storm surges.

Island remains a low-lying limestone shelf, much of it at, or even below, the level of the lake itself. Inundation is prevented only by a circle of dunes and beach ridges. Even farther south, and now a nature reserve, is tiny Middle Island, Canada's most southerly territory. And although only a few hundred hectares in area, it would play a prominent and dark role in the history of Lake Erie.

From Leamington west to almost the mouth of the Detroit River, the cliffs return, although much reduced in height. West of Colchester they dwindle once more, and disappear near the river.

While the waters of Lake Erie have shaped its shores over a long period, those waters can create short-term havoc, as well. It's little wonder that the first written account of the lake likened it to a storm-tossed ocean. Because of its shallowness, strong persistent winds can churn the waters into giant waves in short order. Again, the shallowness also means that the crests of the waves tend to be closer together, making them even more deadly. It is not surprising that these waters hold the bones of so many doomed vessels.

But even the shores are not safe during the lake's fury. Winds that whirl the length of the lake push the water into high surges, which can raise the water level quickly. At times the surges can resemble a tidal wave. On one occasion a four-and-a-half-metre wall of water raced through Buffalo, levelling the homes in an entire neighbourhood and hurtling a schooner several blocks inland. But that is not the end of it. When the winds switch to the opposite direction, as they so often do, the wall of water races back down to the opposite end of the lake, where the water was lowered, and can wreak even more havoc.

But, potentially even more unsettling, beneath the storm-tossed water may lurk the form of Lake Erie's very own "monster" — South Bay Bessie. Said to measure anywhere from five to twenty metres, "Bessie" has been the subject sightings dating as far back as 1793. In the 1870s "Bessie" was again sighted near Buffalo, prompting a posse to gather at the shoreline and begin shooting at anything that moved in the water.[3]

Sightings of "Bessie" (so named in the 1980s) has been reported off and on throughout the twentieth century, enough that the city of Huron Ohio declared itself to be the "live capture control centre" for the monster, while a group of local businessmen offered $150,000 for its capture.

Most sightings have likened Bessie to a large sea serpent, with a snake-like head and, in some accounts, "blazing eyes." In 1993 a fisherman near Port Bruce reported being chased ashore by the thing, while the *Weekly World News* in the same year published a "photo" of the monster wrapped around a sailboat under a headline that read "Monster Sinks Sailboat."

The latest additions to the myth occurred at Port Dover in 2001 when several swimmers reported being bitten by some large, unknown creature. A local doctor who examined the large bites offered the opinion that the attack came, not from a mystery monster, but rather from a bowfin, a large fish that was attempting to protect its own territory.

If Bessie lives anywhere, it is unlikely to be in Lake Erie's "dead zone." This was a region of the lake identified by scientists in the 1970s. The dead zone generally is confined to the central section of the lake where the waters are neither at their deepest nor at their shallowest. Here, while the lowest layers remain cold, the upper layers warm to a degree that they absorb most of the oxygen. As plankton dies, it sinks to the bottom and uses up the little oxygen that remains. Contributing significantly to the dead zone were the excessive amounts of phosphorous being dumped by farms and industries. Stiff new regulations imposed during the 1970s eliminated much of the problem, at least for a time. Then, in the 1990s, the province of Ontario not only ended its pollution-control programs, but simply stopped measuring the phosphorous levels in the lake entirely; cutbacks similar to those that contributed to the E. coli tragedy in Walkerton Ontario.

2

AN "EARTHLY PARADISE"

The First Arrivals

What Lake Erie might have looked like before the last ice age will remain a mystery. The vegetation and the animal life lie buried forever. But once the ice sheets began to finally retreat north of the area, the land bridge at the west end of the lake likely witnessed the passage of animals and the humans that followed them.

Following the retreat of the glaciers, Lake Erie's first human occupants were likely roaming bands of hunters and gatherers belonging to groups who have been named after their weapons, and known as the "Fluted Point" people. Archaeological evidence suggests that they arrived even as the glaciers still hovered only a few hundred kilometres to the north.

Because the waters of Lake Erie were lower at this point, any evidence of these groups in that area now lies below water. As the techniques of sharpening spear points became more refined, the period from 8500 BC to 6000 BC became known as the Plano period. Progressive waves of technical refinements kept sweeping northward, including the development of pottery and pipes. Records place their presence at around AD 1000 But another more advanced group was slowly making its way northward. Known as the Middle Woodland or Mound Builders (due their practice of burying their dead in large mounds) this group practised farming and occupied permanent villages. They are believed to have crossed into Ontario around AD 1300 and were displaced by war or absorption by the earlier occupants.

The Mound Builders belonged to the Iroquoian linguistic group and evolved into the Erie, Petun, and Iroquois nations, as well as the Attiwondaronks and Huron groups, although mound-building itself appears to have ended in Ontario around AD 800.

Much has been written about the Attiwondaronks, or "Atiquandaronk," as the Huron and Iroquois had derisively called them, meaning those who speak strangely. The term they used for themselves was "Onguiaahra," from which it is believed the name Niagara originated. These were the first inhabitants of the Erie shore with whom the earliest Europeans came in contact. Archaeological evidence suggests that they moved into Ontario's southwestern peninsula before AD 1300, settling largely between the Grand River and the Niagara River. South of Lake Erie lived a nation after whom the lake was named, the Ehriehronnons (later shortened to "Erie"), which translates as the "people of the cat" — a reference to the population of panthers that existed at the time.

East of the Niagara River was the land of the Iroquois confederacy, a political union that included the Seneca, the Mohawk, the Oneida, the Onondaga, and the Cayuga. (Later, when the Tuscarora nation joined, they became known as the "Six Nations" — a name they carry to this day.)

North of Lake Erie roamed the Huron, to whom the Attiwondaronks were linguistically related. However, animosity was strong between the Huron and Attiwondaronks on the one side, and the Iroquois on the other. War was never far away. In 1640 the Seneca launched a vicious war against the Attiwondaronks over what they believed was the killing of a Seneca chief named Annenraes. Soon after, when the Iroquois launched their infamous war against the Hurons in 1649 (which featured the notorious torture of the priests Lalemont and Brébeuf), the Attiwondaronks were not spared and by 1653 most of their number had dispersed or been annihilated.

The little that is known of the Attiwondaronks comes from the early French explorers to the region. In 1616, Samuel de Champlain called them the "Neutrals" because of what he perceived to be their refusal to take sides in the traditional wars between the Iroquois and the Huron. Champlain estimated their number at around 4,000 and he observed that they lived by burning trees and planting corn and tobacco in the clearings. Much of Champlain's knowledge is thanks to his interpreter, Étienne Brûlé, who stayed with them during the summer of 1615.

A Recollet missionary named Joseph de La Roche Daillon spent the winter of 1626 with the Neutrals. He recorded that the Neutrals lived in twenty-eight villages, in addition to scattered seasonal hunting and fishing camps. Although the Neutrals moved their villages once the soil became exhausted, the main centre was called Kandoucho, with other villages being named Ong-niaahra (later to become "Niagara") and Teotongniaton. Overseeing them in Daillon's time was a chief named Tsohahissen, or Souharissen, although an earlier chief, while peace still held between the Neutral and the Iroquois, was thought to have been a "queen" named Jikonsaseh.[1]

The next Europeans to record their experience with the Neutrals were the Jesuit missionaries, Fathers Jean de Brébeuf and Joseph Marie Chaumonot. Their remarkable accounts appear in the texts of the *Jesuit Relations,* a document that has proven to provide invaluable insight into the Ontario's aboriginal inhabitants of the seventeenth century. In the ten villages where the two priests stayed they estimated the population to be 3,000, while among the forty overall villages they estimated the population to be 12,000. Theirs was not a happy visit, however, for the Hurons had warned the Neutrals in advance of the illnesses inflicted upon their population by the European diseases borne by the unknowing missionaries. Brébeuf then returned to the mission at Sainte-Marie Among the Hurons where, along with four other fellow priests, he was tortured and killed.[2]

Neutral villages consisted of longhouses made of tree boughs covered with large pieces of bark. The middle of the longhouse would contain as much as a dozen fires, with a family on each side. Excavations at Fort Erie show that the Attawondaronks quarried flint to make arrowheads, spear points, knives, and tomahawks.

While nearly all evidence of the Neutrals has long been eradicated, buried, or ploughed under, a remarkable

Attiwandaronks typically used the longhouse for their dwellings.

remnant known as the Southwold Earthworks, located in Elgin County, has survived. Surrounded by farm fields and forested ravines, the earthworks, a national historic site since 1923, was occupied around AD 1500, and consisted of a double palisade, four to five metres in height with gaps to allow the passage of a stream. Explorations by famed archaeologist Wilfred Jury[3] in the 1940s also unearthed evidence of a succession of villages near Clear Creek. Still earlier, a Chatham amateur archaeologist named Edmund Jones had found the remains of a Neutral village in what is today Rondeau Provincial Park.

While the grisly fate of the Jesuits who were tortured and killed in 1649 still resonated in France and Quebec, the religious fervour to convert the "heathen savages" continued unabated. Next up were a pair of Sulpician priests, one René de Bréhant de Galinée and François Dollier de Casson. Anxious to convert those tribes living west of the Great Lakes, who had yet to encounter their first missionary, the two were in fact part of an exploratory expedition headed by a young Jesuit dropout, René-Robert, Cavalier de La Salle.

Despite farming by the settlers, the Attirondawonk Earthworks have survived and display the trenches used in their palisaded village.

Having read the much sought-after *Jesuit Relations* in France, La Salle hungered for adventure in the new world. During a chance meeting with two Iroquois, La Salle was told of a river that led south of Lake Erie to a faraway salt sea. Imagining that this might at last be the fabled passage to China, La Salle raised enough money to put together an expedition to discover this new route. Governor Daniel de Remy de Courcelle of New France agreed, but only on the condition that he agree to add the two missionaries to his force.

On July 6, 1669, the group set out. Seven canoes, each containing three men and their supplies and equipment, and two Iroquois guides, along with a Dutch settler who was fluent in Iroquois, made their way west along Lake Ontario to an Iroquois village at the end of the lake. Here they met by chance an earlier explorer, Adrien Jolliet.[4] Fresh from Lake Superior, where he was seeking a copper mine, Jolliet told the astonished travellers of a new route to the upper lakes, one that led not through the traditional French River route, but that took him through Lake Erie and Lake Huron.

At this news, the expedition was fated to dissipate. While the two priests decided to follow Jolliet's new route to the north, where more unconverted Natives lay, La Salle took ill and returned to Montreal. This left Dollier and Galinée to become the first to explore and record the shores of Lake Erie. Galinée, it turned out, was a colourful and observant note-taker and his forty-eight-page manuscript has left the earliest account of pre-contact Lake Erie.[5]

On October 4 the little company parted ways, and the priests, with the remaining expedition, made their way west to the Grand River. They found the river very difficult to navigate: "It is marvellous how much difficulty we had in descending the river for we had to be in the water all the time dragging the canoe which was unable to pass through for lack of water."

Ten days later they arrived at the mouth of the river and recorded the first written account of the lake. "At last we arrived on the shore of the lake which appeared to us at first like a great sea because there was a great south wind blowing at the time. There is perhaps no lake in the whole country in which the waves rise so high because of its great depth and great extent." (It is in fact due to the lake's shallowness, not its "great depth" that its waves rise so quickly and steeply.)

During their earlier conversations with Jolliet, the latter had advised them of a canoe he had left along the shore. To secure the canoe for their journey, the priests sent their Dutch interpreter ahead overland to locate it. Setting out into the lake, the expedition struggled for three days with the stormy waters before finally spotting a sheltered landing spot. "We found a spot which appeared to us so beautiful with such abundance of game that we thought we could not find a better place in which to pass our winter." Here they encountered a variety and quantity of game enough to last them the long, cold winter, as well as an ample supply of walnuts, chestnuts, and cranberries. And to their surprise and delight they discovered an abundance of wild grapes. "I will tell you by the way that the vine grows here only in sand on the banks of the lakes and rivers but although it has no cultivation it does not fail to produce grapes in great quantities as large and as sweet as any in France." And they put them to good use. "We even made wine of them with which M Dollier said holy mass all winter."

Galinee wrote glowingly, calling the area "this earthly paradise of Canada." He says: "I call it so because there is assuredly no more beautiful region in all of Canada." The woods were open and the rivers full of fish and game. The "bears [were] fatter and of better flavour than the most savoury pigs of France. In short, we may say that we passed the winter more comfortably than we should have done in Montreal." Despite all the comfort they enjoyed that winter, it would soon change into a series of hardships and discomforts, and, ultimately, failure:

> We could not pass the winter on the lake shore because of the high winds by which we should have been buffeted. For this reason we chose a beautiful spot on the bank of a rivulet about a quarter of a league in the woods. ... At the end of three months our men discovered a number of Iroquois coming to this place to hunt beaver. They used to visit us and found us in a very good cabin whose construction they admired and afterwards they brought every Indian who passed that way to see it ... for that reason we had built it in such a fashion that we could have defended ourselves for a long time against these barbarians if the desire had entered their minds to come to insult us.

The location of this "paradise" was the Lynn River at the site of today's Port Dover, and their winter camp was located on a small stream that flows into it, named Patterson Creek. The earthworks from their winter cabins are visible to this day, fenced and marked with a commemorative cairn.

A cross marks the spot where missionaries Dollier and Galinée celebrated their stay at Port Dover's "earthly paradise."

Finally, after five months and eleven days, on March 29, 1670, they set off again, but not before erecting a cross on a high hill overlooking the lake. But they may have left too soon. After making only six or seven leagues, a strong wind forced them to halt, and they lost a canoe in the process. This forced several of them to walk along the shore to reach where they thought the spare canoe lay waiting. Here they discovered that the shoreline to be frustrating tangle of gullies and underbrush. "We reckoned only two days walking to reach it ... the land route was very bad because of four rivers that had to be crossed and a number of great gulches that the water from the snows and rains had scooped out. We decided it was necessary in order to cross the rivers to go a good distance into the woods because the farther the rivers run into the woods the narrower they are and indeed one usually finds trees which having fallen in every direction to form bridges over which one passes." This worked well until they reached the mouth of Big Creek, which empties into Long Point Bay, (which they termed "Little Lake Erie"). Here, they were forced to fashion a raft, which they guided through the marshy neck of Long Point to the open waters of the lake where "contrary to all expectations found it still quite filled with floating ice."

Eventually they located the canoe and replenished their larder, finding their way to the east side of Point Pelee. Here, they beached their canoes and fell into an exhausted sleep when, during the night, they were suddenly awakened by a terrifying sound. "Astonished to hear the lake roaring so furiously [Dollier] went to the beach to see if the baggage was safe, and seeing that the water already came as far as the packs that were placed the highest point cried out that all was lost."

At this they decided to abandon their mission and return to Montreal. But rather than retracing their exhausting route through Lakes Erie and Ontario, they opted for the by then more familiar route by way of Lake Huron and the French River.

Although they were not likely the first Europeans to see Lake Erie, they have left behind the first written account, a detailed and grim description of that untouched "paradise."

3
THE EUROPEAN INVASION

During the French occupation of Canada, little was happening west of Montreal. This was a time when the government of New France was trying to solidify its trading relationships with the northern tribes such as the Ottawa and the Ojibwa and the southern tribes such as the aggressive Iroquois. Their only built presence in southwestern Ontario were Fort Frontenac at Kingston, Fort Niagara on the south shore of Lake Ontario with its opposite number, Fort Rouille on the site of today's Toronto, while Fort Detroit guarded the entrance to the Detroit River. It was only in this latter location that the government granted lands to French settlers. Their long-lot pattern of farms and their place names survive to this day both within Windsor and throughout the surrounding rural areas of Essex County.

Following the Treaty of Paris, which in 1763 ended of the Seven Years' War (or the French and Indian War, as it was known in North America) between England and France, Britain assumed control over what is today Ontario. During the postwar period the shores of Lake Erie remained quiet. But the American Revolution was soon flaring, and those who had remained loyal to Britain were forced to flee their American homes. As compensation, Britain granted land in New Brunswick and Ontario to those refugees known as United Empire Loyalists. While the first refugees took up their land grants in eastern Ontario in the 1780s, farm lots were being surveyed along the shores of Lake Erie as early as the 1790s. In 1784, Tyendaga chief Joseph Brant was granted all the land along the banks of the Grand River, ten kilometres back, from its mouth at Port Maitland to its source near present-day Dundalk.

But the military presence was never far away. Fort Malden was built between 1796 and 1799 (and known at first as Fort Amherstburg) at the western end of the lake to guard the entrance to the Detroit River, and in 1764, the first Fort Erie had been built to guard the Niagara River on the east. In between, naval reserves were laid out at Port Maitland, Point Pelee, and Turkey Point, where a fort known as Fort Norfolk was started, but hostilities ended before it was completed. But, even as a handful of squatters began to move into such accessible lands as those on Long Point and Point Pelee, the lakeshore's first legitimate settlement scheme was about to unfold.

In 1792, when Colonel John Graves Simcoe arrived in Upper Canada to assume his new duties as governor at Newark (today's Niagara-on-the-Lake, a capital which he soon moved to York), he had with him his private secretary, Lieutenant Thomas Talbot. In 1803, Talbot was granted the authority to issue land grants to prospective settlers in the area east of today's Port Rowan. To help them settle, Talbot ordered the laying out of a road that would extend from Talbotville Royal (today's St. Thomas) to near Point aux

Dressed in period uniforms, the troop at Fort Malden fires off a round, as they might have during the War of 1812.

Pins (Rondeau), near the lake. Much of that route to this day is known as the "Talbot Road."

Talbot was known for being particular as to whom he granted the land. While he rejected many on a whim, he was also considered generous in other ways. He spent his own money to assist many to begin their new lives, would marry them, christen their babies, and conclude his transactions with the passing of a whisky bottle. Still, a parliamentary report in 1834 would raise questions about what happened to the moneys he received for settling the vast tract.

But it was the amount of land that he received that would guarantee his wealth, namely sixty hectares for every twenty hectares he succeeded in granting. By 1820 it was estimated he had acquired fourteen thousand hectares for himself. [1]

Of course, not everyone waited for Talbot to show up for their appointment. United Empire Loyalists had begun showing up as early as the 1780s. They moved along the shoreline and up the small rivers and streams to begin their life in the new land. When water power permitted they threw together first sawmills, and then gristmills. Schooners and skiffs crowded into the little coves and inlets. At first industry was very local, supplying the basic needs of the pioneering communities before they expanded enough to consider exporting.

As the settlements grew, the first exports were raw materials such as gypsum, which were barged from mines on the lower Grand River and transshipped to markets by way of Dunnville and Port Maitland. From the naval reserves, pines tall and straight were sent off to England and the burgeoning Great Lakes shipyards for use as ships' masts. The main lumber export from the shores of Lake Erie, however, consisted of oak, harvested from the lush Carolinian forests and the open oak savannahs, while red cedar from Pelee Island and Point Pelee was popular with the military and used at Fort Malden.

Fishing, which today has become one of the lake's most famous industries, began with local fishermen who simply used small rowboats, known as "punters," from which they would attach pound nets to stakes driven into the shallow waters, and sold their product locally only. Following the arrival of the railways, commercial fishing became centralized in larger ports, while the variety and quantity of fish species turned this freshwater fishing fleet into the world's largest.

Although the lake and the Grand River remained the main thoroughfares for travellers, crude roads also began to appear. Toll roads were extended from London to Port Stanley and from Chatham to Shrewsbury, while the legendary plank road was opened between Hamilton and Port Dover. Thomas Talbot's early Talbot Road already linked St. Thomas with Rondeau.

The war of 1812 halted economic growth in the little lake settlements. Despite early victories at Fort Detroit, the British began to suffer a series of setbacks. At Put-in Bay, near Sandusky, Ohio, despite superior odds, they lost a strategic naval battle. Then, in May 1814, in response to the sacking and burning of Buffalo and Lewiston, American Lieutenant-Colonel Campbell landed with a force of eight hundred men near Port Dover. After allowing the women to carry off their movable items, his soldiers put the torch to the houses, mills, and barns. The hogs were butchered and the meat carried off. The next morning the fleet appeared off Port Ryerse, where the invaders destroyed the mills there and at Finch's Mills (now Fishers Glen).

Later that year, General Duncan McArthur led a force of mounted American riflemen from Detroit along the shore of the lake, burning nearly everything in his path. Strangely, the only mills to escape his wrath were the Backhouse mill north of Port Rowan, and Tisdale's mill at Vittoria — the latter, because, it is suggested that McArthur, a Mason, wished to spare the community of Masons in the area the hardship of losing their vital mill. While the Vittoria mill is now gone, the Backus mill (as it is now called) still rests on its original site and continues to produce flour using the power from its water wheel.

As part of the Backus Heritage Village, the mill also shares the grounds with other heritage structures, as well as summertime campers and picnickers. Run by the Long Point Conservation Authority, the Backus Heritage Village contains more than thirty heritage features that hearken back to pioneer times, including a home built by the Backus family in 1850, as well as a log cabin, bake oven, stump puller, sawmill, and ice house, most brought in from other locations. An ancient cottonwood tree, a Carolinian species, measures thirty metres tall and more than six metres in circumference.

McArthur's devastation of 1814 was complete. From the Detroit River to the Grand, villages, mills, and farms lay in ruin. But the resurrection of the Lake Erie shore would soon begin.

An Industrial Evolution

Following the war, growth began to recur. Homes and mills were rebuilt from scratch. Fields were enlarged and new industries began to appear. Shipping from the little ports increased significantly when in 1825 the Erie Canal was blasted through the rocks of North Tonawanda and into the Niagara River north of Buffalo. This provided not only a direct link between Lake Erie and the Atlantic, but through the Oswego Canal to Lake Ontario, as well.[2] Still, the small size of the canal's locks limited the potential for more shipping. But, in 1833, the Welland Canal opened between Port Dalhousie and Port Colborne with much larger locks.

In 1835, the Grand River Canal facilitated the movement of gypsum, lumber, and barley from the Grand River watershed through Dunnville and Port Maitland, and gave rise to the dozen towns and villages that clustered around the lock stations and shipping docks along the river.[3]

Along the lakeshore, to help encourage exports, the government gave financial encouragement for local landowners to build private wharfs. Often lacking a protective harbour, the wharfs gave rise to a string of now-forgotten little ports with names like Union, Clearville, Port Glasgow, and many that bore only the names of their operators.

South of the border, in the United States, a major population move was under way. Having long suffered under the burden of slavery, American abolitionists, aided by many in Canada, launched the "Underground Railroad." By following a designated route, and resting in safe houses, many fugitive slaves made their way into Canada, with the shore of Lake Erie offering close haven.

The docks at Dunnville shown here when ships still called, now lie beneath concrete and asphalt.

Built in 1846, Lock Number 27 marks the entrance of the feeder canal from Stromness into Lake Erie. It made shipment up the Grand River easier.

Gathering in safe communities on the south shore of the lake, they crossed and settled, usually only temporarily, at Point Pelee, Long Point, Fort Erie, and ports like Shrewsbury, Colchester, Port Burwell, Port Rowan, and Port Stanley. Few, however, remained in these places. After the Civil War in the United States ended in 1865, many returned to family, friends, and a more familiar climate. Others made their way to larger towns and cities where they established themselves, many taking jobs on the growing network of rail lines.

Lake Erie's first major railway line was hammered into the ground in 1854. An American enterprise intended to supply Buffalo with shipments from Lake Huron, the Buffalo and Lake Huron Railway (B&LH) extended from Fort Erie, through Dunnville, Brantford, and Stratford, and on to the shores of Lake Huron at Goderich. It would mark the beginning of a railway era that would dramatically alter the face of the Lake Erie shore.

Soon, more iron links made their way to the shores of the lake. The year before the B&LH opened, the London and Port Stanley Railway (L&PS)

Photo courtesy of Al Patterson.

Port Rowan began to develop after the railway arrived.

began hauling grain and lumber along a short section of track between those two communities. After the Canada Southern (CSR) was completed across the southwestern peninsula in 1873 (essentially an American shortcut between Buffalo and Detroit), branch lines crept southward toward the lake to places like Erieau, Port Rowan, and Port Burwell.

Port Dover boomed with the arrival of the Hamilton and Northwestern Railway (H&NW), a resource line that extended through Hamilton and Allandale (Barrie), and on to the shores of Georgian Bay at Collingwood, while the Lake Erie and Northern Railway (LE&N) from Kitchener to Port Dover provided a second route for that community. Meanwhile, at the western end, Hiram Walker was creating a route from Windsor to Leamington to help bring raw material to his distillery at Walkerville.

By 1880, Walker's steel rails had reached as far as Wheatley, as well. In fact, many of the lake's ports were enjoying the vital rail links, including Erieau, Port Stanley, Port Burwell, Port Rowan, Port Dover, Port Maitland, Dunnville, and Fort Erie. Connecting these ports to vital American markets, car ferries began

Elgin County Archives, Robert Moore Postcard Collection, C6 Sh6 B3 F1 #18.

Railway car ferries shuttled between ports on the Canadian side and those on the American side.

a long era of cross-lake shipping. Erieau, Port Stanley, Port Dover, and Port Maitland benefitted from their links with Ashtabula and Conneaut in Ohio on the American shore. Railcars would be shunted onto the large vessels carrying coal into Canada, and a variety of raw materials into the United States. It was a romantic era that would last well into the 1950s. (The tradition continues to this day with the *Jiiman* and the *Pelee Islander* offering the last cross-lake ferry service linking Leamington and Kingsville with Sandusky. This time, however, the "cars" are not railcars, but automobiles).

A system of radial streetcar lines was emerging, as well, and for the first three decades of the twentieth century they operated to places like Kingsville, Leamington, Port Stanley, Erieau, and Port Colborne.

No industry benefitted more from the arrival of the rails than did fishing. The lake had long been well-known for its quantity and variety of fish such as blue pike, walleye, and whitefish. Natives gathered at places like Long Point for the bounty of the fish. Early on, local fishermen were able to fish close to shore and supply the nearby settlements with a plentiful supply using the simple hook-and-line technique. As settlements and markets grew, linen seine nets came into use as fishing boats grew ever larger. By the 1860s, the seine nets had been replaced by the more efficient "pound" nets,

Punters, such as shown by the harbour at Port Rowan, were used in the early days of fishing on Lake Erie.

allowing the fishermen to cash in on the sudden increase in demand due to the American Civil War.

But the opening of the canals and the extension of the rail lines meant that fishing could now become an export industry. By the 1870s, the rowboats and skiffs were giving way to steam-powered tugs while methods changed from the local pound nets to trawling. Fishing boats became enclosed, allowing for longer trips and for sorting to take place right on deck. During the first two decades of the twentieth century, pound net licenses tripled from 260 to nearly 700 while gill net yardage increased five times from 300,000 to over 1.5 million. In 1915, more than 1,000 fishermen were fishing out of 425 boats.

The invention of the enclosed fishing tug, now in universal use on Lake Erie, helped make the lake's fishery more efficient and more profitable.

Through the late 1800s, lake herring and blue pike were the dominant species. But the lake's fish species faced many challenges: clearing of the land for farming, which altered the water tables and reduced habitat, and the entry of the deadly sea lamprey, an ocean-going predator that literally sucked the life out of any fish to which it attached itself, altered drastically the makeup of the fish stocks. By the 1950s the blue pike was extinct while walleye and whitefish had all but disappeared, leaving yellow perch and rainbow smelt to become the dominant species. Fishing grounds were shifting, as well. Boats in and west of Port Stanley hauled aboard more than 10 million kilograms of fish, while east of Port Stanley, once the lake's most fertile fishing grounds, the haul was less than a quarter of that. And most of that remained at Port Dover, where the catch was almost entirely smelt. The fish most popular in local restaurants, yellow perch, comes from the tugs that operate out of Port Stanley and Erieau. Wheatley, however, has become the most prolific of the fishing harbours, bringing in more than twice the tonnage of any other port and a greater variety, as well. All told, Lake Erie's eleven main fishing ports in 2007 boasted nearly two hundred commercial fishing license holders, a figure that ensures the lake's title as the largest freshwater fishing fleet in the world.

A gas field is under way near Port Burwell, an often forgotten industry on the Lake Erie shore.

Not only did the railways usher in more industry, but a new type of lake user — the tourist. As the Great Lakes area became more urbanized, residents who were crowded into smoky, growing cities sought places to which they could escape. Soon, excursion trains were carrying the throngs to Lake Erie's many sand beaches. Amusement parks sprang up nearly everywhere, some with their own short line trains with colourful names like the Sandfly Express and the Pegleg.

Crystal Beach and Erie Beach on the eastern end attracted Americans in particular, while those at Port Stanley and Port Burwell herded crowds from places like London, and Port Dover largely appealed to vacationers from Hamilton. Soon the Americans were buying up large stretches of shoreline for summer homes, creating private, often gated, communities with their own exclusive station stops.

While the western beaches were scarcer and farther from large urban centres, those at Rondeau, Point Pelee, and Leamington soon boasted hotels and campgrounds and cottages, as well.

Meanwhile, away from the shoreline, agriculture was evolving. By the late 1800s, the traditional mixed-farming economy of wheat and livestock was being replaced with more specialized agriculture. The fertile soils and the warm climates of the extreme southwest was spawning a busy vegetable-growing and greenhouse industry, in particular, tomatoes around Leamington. Tobacco-growing began in the Essex area around the early 1900s and found more fertile ground on the then-depleted sand plains of Norfolk County in the 1920s. Large tracts of marshlands in the Erieau, Turkey Point, and Point Pelee areas, and on Pelee Island, were drained for vegetable-growing.

But fishing, farming, and forestry were not the Erie shore's only industries. A now-forgotten story is that of the oil and gas industry, which operated from 1903 and continues today with offshore rigs. Peat, too, proved the basis for a short-lived iron-making industry at Normandale, west of Port Dover, and for one of Canada's largest peat-extraction industries near Port Colborne.

A New Day Dawns

As the pall of the Second World War receded, major changes began to sweep the Erie shore. This was heralded largely by the arrival of the auto age. While a few cars coughed along the dusty roads of the Erie shore as early as 1900, the postwar years ushered in an overwhelming alteration in lifestyle, industry, and transportation.

By the time the war ended, most of the radial streetcars had been shunted into scrapyards, and the tracks were lifted. A new Welland Canal, completed in the 1930s, was bringing ever-larger boats steaming into the lake. North America's first limited-access freeway was opened by Queen Elizabeth (the Queen Mother) in 1939, while two decades later the 401 (officially known as the MacDonald-Cartier Freeway) was speeding cars and trucks between Toronto and Windsor. Travellers were leaving the trains for the freedom of their own cars, and trucks began taking business away from rail freight. One by one, the rails to the lakes were removed. Today only the tracks to Fort Erie and Port Colborne remain, while the L&PS line has become a tourist line only. Many of the once-busy main lines are now recreational trails.

Then, in the late 1960s, the face of Lake Erie's industry changed yet again. In an effort to decentralize the industrial sprawl plaguing Ontario's large cities, the Ontario government assembled a large tract of land east of Port Dover, luring such heavy industries as Texaco Oil, Dofasco Steel, and Ontario Hydro. This once scenic and idyllic stretch of shore now resembles a gloomy industrial forest. Indeed, the hydro plant is considered to be Ontario's single greatest polluter.

However, clean energy is beginning to dominate the landscape, as well. In an area west of Port Rowan, silhouetted against the sky, are the vast, whirling blades of the sixty wind turbines that make up the Houghton Wind Farm.

Today, condos and cottages clog the shoreline where the amusement parks once bustled. Small industries have moved away, and residents now commute to larger industries in places like Cambridge, St. Thomas, and London.

Even farming itself has changed again. As the demand for cigarettes has declined, the tobacco auction houses have closed and the back-breaking tobacco fields are gradually being replaced with such alternative crops as corn (for ethanol), ginseng, and peanuts, and the dilapidated rows of tobacco sheds now resemble miniature ghost towns. Increasing numbers of farms are converting to pick-your-own operations, and roadside markets line the shore roads. In 1972, the first of the high-bush blueberry farms opened, and that crop has now begun to dominate the roadside and pick-your-own markets.

The cross-lake car ferries have faded into the lake's lore. While fishing remains a major industry, and is still the world's largest freshwater fishing fleet, the focus has changed. While 211 fishing licenses are still issued for boats in eleven harbours, fish are increasingly sold to markets in Toronto and to a growing number of local restaurants. Buying fish fresh from the boats, or at the least in the dockside fish markets, is becoming a popular pastime with the tourist traffic.

Many of the cottages have been cleared from the more sensitive ecological areas, which have become popular destinations for nature-seeking tourists. Beaches are cleaner, and most are crowded during Lake Erie's long, hot summers. The local bed-and-breakfast operations, and the renowned "quaintness" of the old ports are attracting ever more visitors. Indeed, Norfolk County specifically promotes its Lake Erie shoreline as "Ontario's South Coast."

But many other little communities have not benefitted from the busy roads and tourists trade. The schooners no longer call, the mills have long gone with no replacements, and their stores and hotels sit shuttered. Their heydays are only distant memories. These are the places of Lake Erie's "ghost coast."

PART TWO

The Places of the Lake Erie Shore

4
THE BATTLE-SCARRED BOOKENDS

Fort Erie ~ Amherstburg

I n many ways, although they occupy the opposite ends of Ontario's Lake Erie shore, Fort Erie and Amherstburg are almost mirror images of one another. Both began as military towns with forts built to protect the Canadian shore from American attack. Both were major destinations for slaves fleeing the oppression of the United States. Both were among the busiest channels for smuggling booze into the United States during the hated days of prohibition, and both form a terminus for scenic riverside drives.

But there the similarities end. While Fort Erie became a busy crossing point into the United States for both cars and trains, and boasts such attractions as a racetrack, clubs, and modern motels, Amherstburg never realized that potential and has remained, relatively, a backwater. Still, both know how to cherish and celebrate their deep historic roots.

Fort Erie

Fort Erie's first occupants were nomadic groups of Neutral Natives who used the extensive flint beds near the area to fashion arrowheads and spear points. Following the end of the Seven Years' War in 1763, Britain gained control of what had been formerly French territory, and set out to secure the new areas with a series of forts. On the shore of the river, they built a small, wooden fort and store. A small settlement began to slowly take shape along the river, centred around Dunbar's gristmill, built in 1792.

The original wooden fort lasted nearly half a century and was used mainly for transhipping troops and military equipment to the Upper Great Lakes. During the American Revolution the fort continued its role as a supply base for the British. However, its exposure to the fierce winds and waves of the lake caused so much damage that the military embarked on a newer and stronger fort farther from the water.

In 1803, planning began for the new structure, one that would use stone from nearby quarries. But progress was slow, and even by the outbreak of the War of 1812, it remained unfinished. During the war, the partial fort changed hands a number of times, each time being alternately rebuilt or dismantled. The soldiers greatly expanded the fort defences during the American occupation of the site in 1814.

A fierce battle on August 15, 1814, resulted in the loss of 1,000 British troops killed or wounded. The British then began a siege that lasted until September 17, when the Americans finally attacked and destroyed the British gun positions. In November, with the war winding down, the Americans destroyed

Costumed interpreters relive life at Fort Erie during the War of 1812.

the fort and withdrew. Although in ruin, the British occupied the site until the 1820s. The ruins, however, continued to attract attention of would-be invaders such as the Fenians[1], who occupied the site briefly in 1866, but, with its lakeside location, and historic appeal, the ruined fort became a popular attraction for picnickers and visitors, among whom were Mark Twain and the Prince of Wales. In 1937, the federal and provincial governments, and the Niagara Parks Commission, embarked upon a major restoration project. While only a small portion of the stone wall is original, such buildings as the officers' quarters, soldiers' barracks, and powder magazine have been recreated based upon the plans of American occupiers. Today, costumed guides represent the Natives, the troops and the militia of the day along with commissary officer "John Warren" and a "soldier's wife."

But American soldiers were not the only ones crossing the border. In 1793, John Graves Simcoe abolished the importing of slaves into Upper Canada, and began the process of ending slavery in the Canadas. The whole notion of slavery appalled many in the northern United States, where the inhuman benefits of free labour to a plantation economy, as in the American South, held no sway. Outraged abolitionists began to assist slaves in escaping their bonds and resettling in the northern states where they would be free. Southern Ontario, too, became a destination with major terminals being Windsor, St. Catharines, and Chatham, while the key entry points were at Amherstburg and Fort Erie. Because the flow followed set routes, and allowed the escapees to rest at safe houses, or "stations," it became known as the "Underground Railroad."

What at first began as a trickle into Ontario grew into a torrent in 1850 when the American president, Millard Fillmore, signed the notorious Fugitive Slave Act, allowing bounty hunters to capture escaped slaves and making it illegal for Americans to harbour them. Not even free Blacks were safe.

Josiah Hensen, the inspiration for Harriet Beacher Stowe's "Uncle Tom" in *Uncle Tom's Cabin*, recalls in his diaries arriving on the banks of the Niagara River at a large house with pillars. That house still stands. It is Bertie Hall. The basement, unlike most homes, is four metres high, with a secret room hidden behind a moveable bookshelf. From this room it is speculated that a tunnel led the short distance to the riverbank through which the runaway slaves could enter the house undetected. (While there is an anomaly in the masonry on the wall that suggests a tunnel entrance, its existence remains only anecdotal.) The history of Bertie Hall suggests, too, that illicit products also might have found their way through this secret corridor.

The Underground Railroad helped thousands of African-American slaves flee to Canada, using such hiding places as the specially equipped basement of Fort Erie's Bertie Hall.

Harriet Tubman, the legendary "Black Moses," who guided more than five hundred slaves to Canada, mostly to St. Catherines, is said to have used Bertie Hall, as well. The legacy of the Underground Railroad has left more than merely buildings. A series of meetings at a local hotel resulted in the formation of the Niagara Movement, an initiative that eventually evolved into the widely respected NAACP.[2]

Bertie Hall is a stunning building in its own right. Built by William Forsyth between 1826 and 1834 and named after Sir Peregrine Bertie, Duke of Ancaster, it displays the Greek Revival style with pillars stretching to the portico above the front entrance. Forsyth, who had built the Pavilion Hotel at Table Rock in Niagara Falls, one of the cataract's first tourist accommodations, moved to Fort Erie where he acquired an eighty-two-hectare (216-acre) tract of land on the Niagara River.

The house changed hands over the years until it was sold to the Niagara Parks Commission by its last owner, John Killridge, in 1981. Although early

Ferry Landing, Fort Erie, Canada.

Toronto Reference Library, PC ON 587.

Before the Peace Bridge was opened between Fort Erie and Buffalo, ferries provided the main link.

photos show the river literally at the steps of the house, the Niagara Parkway now separates the building from the river. Today it not only houses a basement dedicated to the Underground Railroad, but its upper floors are the site of Mildred M. Mahoney's "Dolls' Houses Gallery," a collection covering two hundred years of dollhouses.

Still, it was not the Underground Railroad that spurred growth at Fort Erie; rather, it was the arrival of the steel ones. Before the railways entered town, what is today "Fort Erie" was little more than a handful of scattered settlements. A few cabins clustered around the fort where ferry service existed as early as 1796 and was known as Fort Erie Rapids. Small Black settlements appeared near Bertie Hall and they came to be known as the Bertie Settlement and Little Africa, clustered along Ridgemount Road near the shipyard, while a third settlement developed at Snake Hill.

Because of its exposure to the lake's often stiff winds, Fort Erie formerly stood in the shadow of a pair of windmills. In 1832, Silas Carter built a twenty-metre (sixty-foot) windmill at what today retains the name Windmill Point. Disused by 1870, only its stone foundation survived. The site is now owned by Buffalo cottagers. In the 1860s, Joseph Wells operated an eight-sided windmill on Wells Hill, a landmark for lake sailors. Following his wife's death in 1890, he tore the structure down.

The year 1853 saw Ontario's first railway, a horse-drawn tramway that served as a portage around Niagara Falls and ran from Chippewa above the falls to Queenston, below the rapids of the Niagara River. In 1857, the line was extended to the ferry docks at Fort Erie and steam engines replaced the horses. By then the settlement was going by the name Waterloo. In 1854, a new line, the Buffalo and Lake Huron Railway (B&LH), was started by American interests and ran from the Fort Erie docks, west along the Erie shoreline, to Dunnville, from which point it then followed the Grand River shoreline to Brantford and on to the shores of Lake Huron at Goderich. In 1855, car ferries were shuttling the rail cars, eight at a time, to the railway's terminus across the river at Black Rock. Waterloo was growing and by 1855 had boomed to a population of nine hundred. The town stretched nearly four kilometres along the river and included four taverns, ten stores, and four churches. It was incorporated as the Village of Fort Erie in 1857 and the name Waterloo disappeared.

In 1870, the Grand Trunk Railway (GTR) absorbed the line and put its chief engineer, Casmir Gzowski, to work building a new bridge to cross the river.[3] Located a short distance north of of the old fort, the bridge attracted a new village, which was at first named Victoria. Near the rail yards west of the bridge, another village was growing and took the name Amigari, where the Grand Trunk located its yards and roundhouse.

But the new International Bridge was attracting other railways, as well, and by 1876, both the Canada Southern and the Canada Air Line were completed and both converged on the new bridge. Again, these new lines served primarily American interests and were little more than short-cuts to Michigan.

From 1873 until 1934, a diminutive streetcar nicknamed "The Dummy" also rattled back and forth over the bridge, providing a local service for commuters and shoppers. But the railway bridge lacked access for pedestrians and motor vehicles. On June 1, 1927, a new road bridge opened to connect Buffalo with Fort Erie, and today the Peace Bridge is Canada's second-busiest border crossing, handling 5.5 million cars and 1.3 million trucks in 2006. Despite the advent of the new crossing, ferries continued to shuttle to Buffalo from the ferry landing at Bertie Street until 1950, as they had since 1796. A plaque in Freedom Park commemorates the longevity of this historic crossing point.

To honour the bridge of peace, the Mather Arch forms the centrepiece of a memorial garden and monument to the bridge and the nations it unites and

A memorial to Alonzo Mather celebrates his encouragement for the building of the Peace Bridge between Fort Erie and Buffalo.

"to signify the blessings of lasting peace and (the) friendship and goodwill (that) bridge the frontier between these two nations." The park is in honour of Alonzo Clark Mather [4], an industrialist, who, in 1919, initiated the drive to construct such a bridge.

Victoria and Amigari amalgamated and became Bridgeburg and grew around the rail yards. Meanwhile, Fort Erie, having lost its railway terminals, began to dwindle. Eventually it benefitted from Bridgeburg's growth and in 1932 both joined under the name Fort Erie. Later, the Canada Southern came into the fold of the Michigan Central Railway, which along with the GT, added a station near the bridge. While that of the GT was an elegant building with a conical roof above the waiting room (known as a "witch's hat"), that of the MC was typical of American lines, a much simpler brick design.

Downstream from the railway bridge, a busy shipyard became the focus for a small settlement known as Bridgeburg Shipyard, and a station on the Ontario and Lake Erie Railway. From 1904 until 1930, three companies built a number of ships, including four ocean cargo boats, as well as the *War Magic* and the *War Vixen*, which plied the ocean between 1917 and 1919. A marina opened in 1965 and the pleasure boats of today occupy the two wide slips of the former shipyards. Today it remains the site of Millers Marina and now also the Dockside Grille. A plaque on the path of the Parkway bike trail depicts the history of this forgotten site.

Bridges were not needed for another of the town's clandestine "industries." Between 1919 and 1930, Fort Erie developed into one of the main transits for "rum-running" during the American prohibition. Motorboats would make their way to the middle of the river from the Canadian side, loaded with cases of beer, whisky, and port, and there offload their contraband into smaller rowboats, which could, if the speedy coast guard closed in on them, hurl their contraband into the water more quickly than larger boat.

In 1941, the Queen Elizabeth Way (QEW) was extended from St. Catharines to Fort Erie, although it remained unpaved for the duration of the war. In 1956, the Fort Erie link of the QEW was finally paved and opened to the Peace Bridge — turning the one-time railway town into the second-busiest border crossing in Canada. Ironically, the new bridge has attracted most of today's new growth to the old section of Fort Erie, while the commercial core of what the merchants call "Bridgeburg Station" struggles to survive.

The heritage of the town has experienced mixed success. The old town hall and several of the original hotels have been removed, while the CN tore out the attractive GT station in 1973. Happily, however, the town bought the Michigan Central station for $1.25 and moved it to the grounds of the railway museum, where it shares its heritage with the former Ridgeway station and CN's steam locomotive number 6218. Around it most of the tracks and roundhouse and yards are gone and lie overgrown. At the northwest corner of the town, Amigari remains a separate nucleus of small homes on a traditional railway-style grid network of narrow, rugged streets. While the yards remain, no railway buildings, or original buildings from the early days of rail activity, have survived.

Gone too is the Erie and Niagara line, as have the tracks of the Canada Southern, which have been replaced now with a hiking and cycling trail. The Canadian Pacific and Canadian National railways, however, still run freight trains across Gzowski's historic bridge. In addition to Fort Erie and Bertie Hall, historic plaques erected by the Niagara Parks Commission commemorate the shipyards and the sites of the early ferry landings.

Amherstburg

While this westernmost of Lake Erie's Ontario towns has much in common with its eastern twin, much also differs.

Following the American Revolution, when the 1783 Treaty of Paris turned the British Fort Detroit over to the Americans, the British needed another military post to guard the strategic waters of the Detroit River. At a site where the river enters the lake, in 1796, they built Fort Amherstburg. During the American incursion in 1813, the British vacated the fort, destroying it as they did.

During their own occupation of the ruins between 1813 and 1815, the Americans began to rebuild. With the war's end in 1814, the construction stopped, and when the British showed up in 1815, they continued the repairs on what was now called Fort Malden after the township in which Amherstburg is located. During the 1820s, plans were drawn up for new buildings, but few were completed. Finally, with border tensions easing, the British vacated the fort in 1836.

But they returned almost immediately, for in 1837, the Upper Canada rebellion had broken out. Two large barracks, officers' quarters, a jail, and various artillery buildings were hastily erected. But by the 1840s the need for such a post had once more dwindled, and in 1851, the soldiers marched out yet again, this time for good. In 1859, the Ontario government acquired the site for a mental health facility, converting the fort's structures into patient housing and adding a two-storey brick laundry. When the facility closed in 1879, the site became a lumberyard and the grounds were divided up for housing.

Reconstruction of the site by Parks Canada has turned the fort into a heritage attraction, although few of the original structures remain, only a brick barracks and the hospital laundry building. Nevertheless, the earthworks have been restored to their 1840s condition and the foundations of many of the military buildings excavated and marked, among them the cookhouse, ordnance shed, and officers' quarters. Today, as the "redcoats" replay musket drills for tourists, the laundry contains displays, while the barracks have been restored to display period furnishings.

About the same time as the first fort appeared, the town of Amherstburg was being laid out. By 1817, it contained 106 houses strung along the river. In 1850, gazetteer author William Smith commented that Amherstburg "is for Canada an ancient place … It has a very old-fashioned look to it, most the houses being built in old French styles. The streets are narrow and sidewalks paved with stone. It was incorporated as a village in 1851 and became a popular tourist destination with five hotels and ferries which linked it with Windsor, Detroit and other Lake Erie ports."[5]

Amherstburg's narrow streets indicate that its layout is an old one.

In 1874, a fire raced through the town, gutting or destroying many of its finest old buildings, especially those along Murray Street. However, the main river road, Dalhousie Street, escaped much of the holocaust.

During the days of the Underground Railroad, Amherstburg was a key destination for fleeing American slaves. Most, however, would continue inland, many making their way to William King's Elgin Association Settlement at North Buxton near Chatham. Here, unlike in many of the Black settlements, King divided the land to be held individually rather than communally — a strategy that turned his scheme into a rare success story. To this day, the majority of that community's residents trace their roots to the Underground Railroad. Many others headed for Windsor, while a large community remained in Amherstburg, establishing the Nazrey African Methodist Episcopal Church.

As along much of the Detroit River during Prohibition, brazen rum-runners dodged the coast guard and police. While most of their booty crossed between Windsor and Detroit (especially since the Walker distillery was nearby), Amherstburg offered the advantage of being a backwater and having several islands in the river to help conceal the illicit activities. Contemporary photos published in the Detroit newspapers show concealed rum boats tied up at Amherstburg's export docks ready to haul their load to their "posted" destinations of Mexico or the Caribbean.

While railways converged on Fort Erie, they avoided Amherstburg. Only a branch line of the Michigan Central Railway made its way into town from Essex. Although proposals were touted for a bridge across the river to link the Gordon Dock north of town with Wyandot on the American side, only the concrete abutments were ever built, and they remain visible today. The Michigan Central station, built in 1896, however, has managed to survive, and although the tracks have long been lifted, the station retains its external appearance, while inside, the popular Gibson Art Gallery displays many local and renowned works of art. It is owned by the Fort Malden Guild of Arts and Crafts and is known for its annual Art by the River arts and crafts show, the county's oldest such event.

Despite the devastation of the 1874 fire, Amherstburg contains some of Ontario's oldest buildings. The Park House, now a museum, was first built by Loyalists on the American side of the river near the River Rouge, which is tributary of the Detroit River. The anti-Loyalist rage that followed the revolution forced the family to dismantle their home and have it towed it downstream to Amherstburg in 1798. Thomas Park bought the house in 1839 and, with his family, operated a number of business ventures from it, including a general store and shipping operation. The house remained in the Park family until 1941. For the next twenty-nine years it functioned variously as apartments and an antique store. In 1970, new owners threatened to demolish the house. Being considered the oldest house in the area, a movement was quickly launched to save it and move it, and in 1973 it took up its new location as a museum just off Dalhousie Street in the town's historic core.

Nearby stands the Gordon House. Built in 1798, it too was threatened with demolition in 1982 and was moved to its new site near the Park House. Now restored, it houses the Town of Amherstburg Tourism and Special events office, the chamber of commerce, and a wine festival office.

Just behind the historic main street, located within King's Navy Yard Park, sits what was built in 1831 as the office for Commissariat Office for Fort Malden. Today it functions as an educational centre of marine history.

The story of the Underground Railroad is told in the North American Black Historical Museum and cultural centre located on King Street. Beside it is the Nazrey African Methodist Episcopal (AME) Church, now a national historic site. Escaped slaves and free blacks toiled with fieldstones to build the church in 1848 so that traditional AME congregations need not risk returning to their former church congresses in the United States.

While the streets of downtown Amherstburg retain their narrow aspect and historic ambiance, the most spectacular single building lies about a kilometre to the south, and is known as the Bellevue House. Built in 1816, this sprawling white mansion is described as one of the finest remaining examples of domestic Georgian architecture in Ontario. It was home to Robert Reynolds, the commissary to the garrison at Fort Malden, and to his sister, Catherine Reynolds, who became one of Canada's best-known landscape painters. Despite its status as a national heritage site, the property today stands vacant, in need of paint, while its yard succumbs to weeds.

Scenic river routes lead both north and south of Amherstburg until they become obscured by riverside development. Perhaps its status as something of a backwater is a boon to Ontario's heritage lovers, for little has occurred to obscure the deep history of this old and vital riverside community.

5
THE AMERICANS ARE COMING (AGAIN)

Erie's Playgrounds

Erie Beach ~ Crystal Beach ~ Bob-Lo Island

The contrast between the Canadian and American sides of the Niagara River at Fort Erie, and of the Detroit River couldn't be more dramatic. While in both cases the American shores have long been lined with heavy industry and congested cities, the Canadian shores have remained cleaner and more lightly developed, a surefire lure for hot, weary tourists from "south of the border." (Actually, "east" of the border, as in the case of Buffalo, and "north" of the border, as in the case of Detroit.)

The Ghosts of Erie Beach

One of the earliest stretches of Lake Erie to fall to the Americans was a sandy stretch of shoreline a short distance west of the site of an earlier American conquest, the fortifications of Fort Erie. Here, a park, known originally as the Snake Hill Grove, the one-time site of a major battle during the War of 1812, was started by Buffalo entrepreneurs Benjamin and Edward Baxter, and W.R. Pierce. Sand-seeking Buffaloneans would travel to Fort Erie where they would board the little narrow gage train, the "Sandfly Express," officially known as the Fort Erie Snake Hill and Pacific Railroad. (The addition of the word "Pacific" was no doubt a satirical reference to the practice of many a resource railway to optimistically add "Pacific" to their charter name). New equipment was bought from the New York elevated steam railway in 1901 and the little line operated until the park closed in 1930.

Crumbling piers mark the location where vacationers would disembark from the Buffalo boats to enjoy the rides at the Erie Beach Amusement Park.

The popular amusement park boasted a hotel, casino (in those more moral days, a "casino" was usually a dance hall, and not a gambling establishment), boardwalk, rides like the Lind Loop, and carousels, as well as entertainment, which featured diving horses, Olympic athletes, boxing, and Mack Sennett's "bathing beauties."[1]

In 1930, the park closed and was purchased by the owners of Crystal Beach Park, to prevent, it is speculated, new competition from being built on the site. They succeeded better than they ever would have thought. The hotel burned in 1935, while the building that contained the casino stood in ruin until 1975, when it was declared dangerous and torn down.

Over several years, trees and shrubs have slowly reclaimed the site. Al Sobol, in his entertaining book, *Looking for Lake Erie*, found disintegrating walls, a crumbling pier, and jagged pieces of concrete. Today, the forest covers a ghostly site of concrete slabs and a network of crumbling sidewalks, while a pair of concrete piers, where the Buffalo steamers once called, is slowly being reclaimed by the lake's crashing waves. A new walkway, the Friendship Trail, traces the route of the old boardwalk along the shore of the lake where many of the concrete ruins remain clearly visible. Access to the trail is through Waverley Beach Park at the end of Helena Street.

Crystal Beach's Condo Canyons

Before Canada's Wonderland opened its state-of-the-art park north of Toronto in 1982, Crystal Beach, halfway between Fort Erie and Port Colborne, was the place to go for a summer of thrill rides.

It didn't begin that way, though.

The site was first opened in 1888 as a religious camp modelled on the Chautauqua concept[2] then popular in North America. (Another such park was located at Grimsby Beach near Hamilton.) An assembly house at the corner of Derby and Erie Roads, today the centre of the town of Crystal Beach, lured the throngs for their lectures. Gradually, amusements on the periphery of the grounds were added to provide a diversion for the children while the adults soaked up the sermons. Soon the fresh air, a shallow sandy beach, and the ambience of the grounds were attracting 150,000 visitors each year.

In 1890, recognizing a profitable opportunity when they saw one, a group of Buffalo investors formed the Crystal Beach Company and began to install

Ontario Archives, RG 1-G-54.

The steamship Canadiana *arrives at the Crystal Beach pier.*

more amusement rides and refreshment booths. For three years, they ran a monorail-style elevated railway, known as the Pegleg, from the Ridgeway station on the Grand Trunk line to the grounds. Running on a tramway that stood up to fourteen metres above ground in places, the single twenty-passenger coach was powered by an electrical cable and could reach speeds of forty kilometres per hour. More properly known as the Ontario Southern Railroad, it lasted only three years, as visitors stuck to the more reliable steamship service from Buffalo. A midway and more rides were added and by 1910 the park had expanded to four times its original size. The same year, two new passenger ferries, the *Americana* and the *Canadiana*, were put into service with capacities of 3,500 and 2,700 passengers respectively.

The park was purchased by the Buffalo and Crystal Beach Corporation in 1924. About this time, a new village was laid out north of the park with

A postcard view of the Crystal Beach midway during the amusement park's heyday.

narrow streets radiating out from a central park. The park would soon boast what was considered North America's largest unobstructed dance hall. Here the 3,500-square-metre Crystal Ballroom hosted such bands as Artie Shaw, the Dorsey Brothers, Gene Krupa, Glenn Miller, and, of course, Ontario's own Guy Lombardo and His Royal Canadians.[3]

Even during the Depression, Crystal Beach Park grew and prospered. Following the the Second World War, parking was expanded and the rides were upgraded with still more new thrills added. But at the same time, the big bands were replaced with smaller rock groups. The ferry service ended in 1956. As a result, traffic jams increased and attendance shrank.

Crystal Beach was also showing its age, and none too gracefully. New amusement parks, more modern in concept, opened at Canada's Wonderland, as well as Darien Lake in New York State, and Marineland and Game Farm in Niagara Falls, Ontario. The park struggled on, but its fate was inevitable. Even the introduction of a 1920s vintage heritage ferry service couldn't save it. On Labour Day, 1989, the park fell silent.

Since that time, a $60-million gated condo development has taken over the site, while many of the stores and fast food joints along Derby Street now sit boarded up, their sidewalks overgrown, others are altering their selections to cater to the new arrivals. All that remains of the popular beach itself is a

A wall of condos lines the water's edge at Crystal Beach, where the remains of the holiday pier can still be seen.

small day-use park and boat launch site known as Crystal Beach Park. With no signs to point to it, the park lies hidden away at the end of Ridgeway Road. From the park the view extends to the long, crumbling pier where the steamers once called, and the wall of condominium townhouses which have been built right to the very edge of the seawall. Far to the east of the park, the skyscrapers of Buffalo loom above the horizon, while to the west lies Point Abino and at its tip the lighthouse that has caused much controversy. (See Chapter 10.)

The Crystal Beach urban area, however, continues to grow, and has now virtually merged with the community of Ridgeway while the small once-seasonal cottages on the narrow streets are often owned by permanent dwellers.

Crystal Beach lies thirteen kilometres west of Fort Erie and three kilometres south of Highway 3.

Bob-Lo Island

In much the same way that the Americans "invaded" Crystal Beach and Erie Beach at the east end of the lake, a similar incursion was occurring at the west end. Just off shore from Amherstburg lies Bois Blanc Island. A mere five kilometres long, and less than one kilometre wide, the island was strategic from the days of the earliest European contacts. In the 1700s it was the site of a Catholic mission to the local tribes, and, with the establishment of Fort Amherstburg, became a busy campsite for tribes congregating to trade with the British. Among them was the Shawnee chief Tecumseh who fought so valiantly with the British during the war of 1812.

During the rebellion of 1837, the British added three blockhouses to help defend what was then Fort Malden on the mainland and a lighthouse to guide the rapidly growing lake traffic away from the sandbars and shoals. In January of 1838, a force of "patriots" invaded the island, forcing the small military garrison and the lighthouse keeper to flee and then plundered their home. When the band tried to land at Fort Malden, their vessel ran aground, and the rebels were quickly captured.

Once the British departed Fort Malden, they no longer needed the Bois Blanc defences and by mid-century had sold the island to the local member of Parliament, Arthur Rankin. He sold it in turn to his son, Arthur McKee Rankin, then a rising theatrical star who built a large home there, stocking the island with deer. Rankin then sold the estate to John Atkinson and James Randall, who in 1898 found willing buyers in the Detroit, Belle Island, and Windsor Ferry Company, a Detroit-based company anxious to supplement its transportation revenue with an amusement park.

The new American "invasion" was underway. By 1903, the island could boast a carousel and a dance hall built by Henry Ford. Soon, steamers were carrying boatloads of picnickers from Detroit to the open spaces and fresh air of what was now being called "Bob-Lo" Island, as the non-francophone Detroiters pronounced it.

In 1949, the family-owned Browning Steamship Company bought the park and added rollercoasters, a ferris wheel, a miniature railway, a zoo, and upgraded the docks. After the Brownings sold the island in 1979, its reputation declined, culminating with a 1987 roundup of members of the notorious Outlaws Motorcycle Club. After Labour Day 1991, the amusement park on Bob-Lo fell silent.

The Bob-Lo Island amusement park has been replaced with a new housing development.

In 1961, the federal government declared the lighthouse a national historic site for its role in the aborted 1837 rebellion. Built of stone in the "Imperial tower" style, it was automated as early as 1927. Now lantern-less, the lighthouse now belongs to Parks Canada's lengthy roster of important historic properties. The rest of Bob-Lo Island, meanwhile, is surging back to life as an exclusive residential housing development. While a modern ferry shuttle operates from a new dock, the sagging remains of the old dock remain visible from the shore near the Bellevue House.

6

THE CANAL TOWNS

Port Colborne ~ Port Maitland ~ Stromness ~ Dunnville

T hree historic communities cluster near the mouth of the Grand River and, despite their distance from it, all have historic links to the Welland Canal, as well to a less well-remembered canal, that which followed the Grand River itself. Meanwhile, at the Lake Erie terminus of the Welland Canal, Port Colborne remains a functioning port, and contains one of Ontario's more unusual main streets, and a former private enclave of wealthy American southerners.

Port Colborne

Despite their hypnotic grandeur, the thundering falls of Niagara, to all intents and purposes, posed a transportation nightmare. Combined with a long gorge of fierce rapids and the steep cliffs of the Niagara Escarpment, they remained a major impediment to moving people and products and hindered the development of Lake Erie's shoreline communities. No wonder the most-travelled corridor continued to be via the Ottawa and French Rivers.

Following the opening of the Erie Canal to Tonawanda, north of Buffalo, in 1827, the British decided they needed their own link between Lake Ontario and Lake Erie. One of the chief instigators of a new canal, which would be entirely on Canadian soil, was William Hamilton Merritt. In 1828, his project was realized and the first Welland Canal opened for shipping from Port Dalhousie on Lake Ontario as far as Port Robinson, near the town of Welland, from which point it followed the Welland River to Chippewa on the upper

Niagara River. In 1833, it was completed to Gravelly Bay on Lake Erie, where a busy town would develop and be known as Port Colborne.

Prior to that, a small village had begun to develop around Sugarloaf Hill, where in 1781, one of the area's first settlers, Christian Zavitz, erected the area's first vital gristmill. In 1854, the Buffalo and Lake Huron Railway added a station by the canal and was shortly thereafter linked with the rails of the Welland Railway. A third railway, a horse-drawn streetcar line, known as the Toronto and St. Catharines Railway, evolved into a radial streetcar line between Port Dalhousie on Lake Ontario with Port Colborne. In 1853, the canal was enlarged, and again in 1887. When, in 1932, the canal was modernized, turning Port Colborne's old stone locks into a backwater.

The port developed in several sections. The original settlement of Humberstone, about three kilometres north of the lake, developed at Stone Bridge,

Port Colborne's historic lift bridge is one of the last such bridges in Ontario.

where Sherk Road and Chippawa Road met. The first rail junction was located on the east side of the canal (where the controversial INCO smelter would choose to locate, as well). But the main growth was along the west side of the canal and was known as West Street. With its string of historic old stores and its location along the canal, West Street presents an image as one of Ontario's more unusual main streets. The port also attracted a pair of grain elevators, the Johnson elevators, at the mouth of the harbour, and the Robin Hood mills situated above the first set of locks.

One of Port Colborne's largest industries has also been one of its most controversial. In 1918, the International Nickel company of Canada (INCO) established a large nickel refinery east of the canal where a townsite for its 2,400 employees was laid out. In the 1990s, after the refinery had ceased refining nickel, the residents of the townsite discovered high concentrations of nickel copper and cobalt in their soils and launched a lawsuit against INCO, the Ministry of the Environment, the Region of Niagara, and the Town of Port Colborne. They claimed their health was being threatened by the mineral levels, which a government study showed was higher than standards allowed. The amount being claimed was $750 million.

Although further studies seemed to indicate that the contamination was not enough to pose a health risk, the government ordered INCO to clean up twenty-five polluted properties in the townsite. That has not deterred the litigants, however, and in September 2008, a judge set October 2009 as a date for the lawsuit to be heard. The plant halted its refining activities, and now with a workforce of just two hundred, is involved in the processing and warehousing of electrolyte nickel from Thompson, Manitoba.

With its many canal-related buildings, Port Colborne contains one of the best collections of heritage buildings along the Lake Erie shore. It's hard to know where to begin, but the canal forms the strongest focus. Besides the old locks themselves, there is the vertical lift bridge. Built in 1929, it has a span of eighty metres and a clearance of forty metres when raised. Using counterweights to provide the heft, it is the last functioning vertical lift bridge south of St. Catharines. Beside the bridge, the stonework of the early locks still shows the skill of the canal builders, while ships inch beneath the bridge and into the confines of the new canal. The new lock, known as Lock Number 8 (they are numbered from the lowest to the uppermost), is in fact a "guard" lock. Rather than lowering the flow itself, it simply adjusts the level of the canal to the changing level of the lake.

Railways still run to the grain elevators in the harbour, and, as they do, they pass the former CN rail station. Built in 1925, it also served the streetcar system. When it was no longer needed by CN it sat disused and later became a popular local restaurant. As of this writing, it awaits a new owner.

The stores on West Street provide an ideal setting for a stroll and a bit of shopping. One of the most eye-catching is that of the Imperial Bank of Canada. Built in 1911, it displays a unique terra cotta exterior in the beaux-arts style. Other structures include the L.G. Carter General Store at 230 West Street, which was built in 1851, while at number 62, the former Lakeview Hotel dates back to 1840.

Some of the town's finest old homes can be found along King Street, Catharine Street, and Fielden Avenue, where the magnificent Roselawn house sits. It was built in a Second Empire style originally for Levi Cornwall in 1860. But one of the most significant structures is the simpler two-storey stone house found at 44 King Street. Built in the 1840s, it was originally owned by the builder of the canal himself, William Hamilton Merritt.

The most interesting part of town, however, harboured yet another of those American enclaves. In 1888, an organization of American southerners from Memphis founded the Humberstone Summer Resort Company, otherwise known as Solid Comfort Grove. Here, on a sandy stretch of shore west of the harbour they built twenty-five grand summer homes which they would reach by stage from their exclusive station on the Grand Trunk Railway. To further ensure that exclusivity, when they entered the property they would shut a pair of large stone gates behind them. The resort hosted many American dignitaries, including Mrs. Jefferson Davis, widow of the former president of the Confederate States of America. The resort boasted its own bowling alley and in 1912 added a "casino." When the club folded in 1933, and no one showed up to pay the taxes, the town took over the properties.

Unlike during the active days of the resort, these gates now remain open, and have become a designated heritage structure. Slung between two limestone pillars, the original wrought-iron gates were built in 1898, and donated to the town by the O'Fallon family, who named the pillars after their daughters, Elizabeth and Caroline. While many new homes now line what is today called Tennessee Avenue, the most visible building inside the gate is the

Tennessee Avenue's former casino is one the street's most historic homes.

former casino with its three large and distinctive hip gables over the ends and over the portico.

Port Colborne was also home to one of Ontario's forgotten industries — the extraction of peat. In 1894, eight hundred hectares of a marsh, known as the Wainfleet Bog, was sold to the Ontario Peat Company. Sweating labourers would cut the peat into squares in the summer and place them on a narrow railway that hauled the blocks to the Atkinson and Dunn factory at the fringe of the bog. (During the Second World War this toil was put on the backs of German prisoners of war.) The summer was spent stacking the peat, the winter processing it. Later, the company became the Erie Peat Company.

In 1988, the Ministry of Natural Resources purchased over two hundred hectares of the bog for natural regeneration, turning administration over to the Niagara Region Conservation Authority. A small parking area by the site of the former factory allows visitors access to view wildlife, following what was the right-of-way of the tiny railway. Here and there in the woods lie twisted rails and rotting culverts from the days of the railway. Until recently, one of the little peat cars stood near the parking lot, but has since been removed. But, deeper in the woods, a vigilant searcher can still discern a few rotting carcasses of some of those railcars.

Port Maitland

Port Maitland is a split community. Located at the mouth of the Grand River, the section of town that lies on the east side is separated from its neighbours on the west by the river itself, here about half a kilometre wide. The older of the two portions is that on the east side. In 1815, the British surveyed out a naval reserve here, as the bloodshed from the War of 1812 was still fresh and hostilities could resume at nearly any time.

By 1816, the reserve buildings included a blacksmith shop, a kiln, a cabin for the commandant, a barracks that measured eight metres by six metres for the shipwrights, military barracks, a surgeon's quarters, and a grand home measuring eighteen metres by seven metres for Captain Montresors. In all, the entire village consisted of twenty-two buildings.

Even as the military role was winding down, Port Maitland was about to take on a new role. In 1833, the Welland Canal had entered the lake at Port Colborne on Lake Erie, but needed an additional source of water. A feeder canal was extended from Welland to Dunnville where the Grand River had been dammed. From a turning basin nearby, it also continued to the mouth of the Grand where, at Port Maitland, Lock Number 27 was added. By 1840, however, the military had left and the naval buildings sat in ruin. But the port continued to grow as a shipping point for lumber, much of which was shipped to the United States following the Great Chicago Fire of 1871.

After the extension of the Toronto, Hamilton and Buffalo Railway to Port Maitland in 1916, a railcar ferry service began between the port of Ashtabula, Ohio. This gave the TH&B its much-desired access to the American ports on Lake Erie, which it was unable to get through its main line to Welland.

On board the ship, the *Maitland 1*, railcars, filled with coal destined for the steel plants in Hamilton, would arrive at the Port Maitland dock. After the coal cars rattled off the decks, the ferry would load up with newsprint for the American shore. When a newer and larger Welland Canal opened in 1932, the rationale for the car ferry ended and the ship was laid up. In 1935 it was leased out to a Michigan company and continued to operate until 1977, ending its days as a pulpwood barge.

Throughout the 1950s, the port was considered to have Lake Erie's largest fishing fleet. Soon after, many of the vessels moved on to Port Dover, giving that community the honour of hosting the "largest" fleet, a title that now

TOP: *The historic lighthouse on the Port Maitland pier still guides ships into the Grand River estuary. BOTTOM: Port Maitland. The TH&B station at Port Maitland served local industry until it was removed in the early 1990s.*

belongs to Wheatley. Today, Port Maitland's fleet now numbers only a handful of tugs with the Wayne Siddall Fisheries.

While cottages and summer homes now occupy the site of the old naval reserve, new industry has arrived, as well, and Innophos continues to use the spur line of the TH&B, although the old station, originally a residence, was removed in the 1990s.

The only historical legacy of the east shore lies in the stone walls of Lock Number 27, where an historical plaque and information board outline the history of the port and present historic views of the locale. Efforts are underway to celebrate and preserve these ancient lock structures.

Meanwhile, the west portion of Port Maitland is the more residential portion. Here, the breakwater extends well into the lake, and the Port Maitland lighthouse occupies its very tip. Built in 1871, the lighthouse replaced the original wooden structure that was blown into the lake during one of Lake Erie's many tempests. A park lines the river from the pier to the older section of

Although it no longer boasts the lake's largest fishing fleet, Port Maitland retains its fishing heritage.

the village a short distance upstream. Closer to the lake, newer homes both permanent and seasonal have been added, although the early homes of the fishermen can still be seen on the lanes which lead away from the river. It is here too, on nearby Lighthouse Drive that the little stone Christ Anglican Church contains a grave with the remains of twenty-five souls who drowned on May 6, 1850, when the *Commerce* went down just off the shore.

Port Maitland East lies at the end of Haldimand Road 64, just west of Road 3, while Port Maitland West can be found at the end of Haldimand Road 11, about seven kilometres south of Dunnville.

Dunnville

Despite its location upstream from Port Maitland, Dunnville is historically and geographically a Lake Erie port. With no rapids or falls below it, Dunnville is in effect the head of navigation on the Grand River.

Its history, however, predates that role. In 1784, the Haldimand Deed granted to Joseph Brant, a Tyendinaga chief, and the Mohawks who accompanied him to Canada, a ten-kilometre strip of land on both banks of the Grand River from its mouth to its source.[1] But, to gain a source of revenue for his impoverished band, Brant began to sell and lease his holdings. In 1798, more than 140,000 hectares were gone. The same year, Benjamin Canby, an early settler, acquired 7,600 hectares, part of which contained the future site of Dunnville.

William Anthony, another early settler, built one of the region's first mills in 1825. A small settlement grew up on the southwest bank around them and was named Anthony's Mills. Later renamed Byng, to honour British Admiral Byng, the settlement contained not just mills, but Kennedy's log tavern. On the opposite shore, Solomon Miner, said to be the community's first citizen, laid out what would become Dunnville. The completion of a dam in 1829 made the location ideal for the terminus of the Welland Canal's much-needed feeder canal. Dunnville chose its name to honour John Henry Dunn, president of the Welland Canal Company and receiver general for Upper Canada.

Early on, a string of hotels was built along the canal at the point where it merged with the Grand. In 1835, the Grand River canal opened, and Dunnville became an important point for the transhipment of products between the larger lake vessels and the smaller schooners and barges that plied the shallow waters and narrow locks of the Grand River Canal. Queen Street developed as the main commercial core through town, while some of the grander homes would appear along Alder and Broad Streets.

Dunnville attracted a textile industry and in 1907 was home to four large textile mills. The last, Wabasso Limited, survived until 1987 when it closed, bringing to an end an important chapter in Dunnville's economic history.

Another era was that of the railway. In 1854, the Lake Erie and Huron railway (LE&H) built a station, but another sixty years would pass before Dunnville received its second railway, a branch of the Toronto Hamilton and Buffalo (TH&B), which led to Port Maitland. By the 1880s, the Grand Trunk was operating the LE&H line and built an elaborate structure with a pair of towers to decorate its roof. It stood near Cedar and Forest Streets. It burned and was replaced with a small, simple building, which lasted until the tracks were lifted in the late 1980s. The TH&B line, meanwhile, stayed well to the east of town before curving along the bank of the river on its way to Port Maitland. Although its original station has gone, its replacement still remains. A 1950s modernist structure, it stands on the south side of Main, having been converted to a car dealership.

Although the canals have long fallen silent and the GT line is gone, Dunnville is anything but a backwater. Highway 3 hums as a main traffic artery,

The Grand Trunk built a fanciful station at Dunnville. It burned and was replaced by a simpler structure, which also burned.

linking Fort Erie and Port Colborne with Tillsonburg and St. Thomas. Queen
Street bustles with shoppers, and highway commercial development stretches
along Main Street and Broad Street.

Despite the canal's having been been filled in to allow an extension of
Main Street, much remains from the town's historic days. Streets with names
like Market and Front Street, located south of Main, testify to their early roles
as canal-side streets. Today, only a few small, early homes remain. Many of
the more significant heritage structures, however, stand along Queen Street
where, at Queen and Main, the Queens Hotel dates back to 1840. Near
Chestnut and Queen, Ramsey's Men's Wear, which has been around for over
ninety years, occupies the town's oldest building, a commercial structure
built in 1834. Most of the other buildings in the downtown area date from
the later 1800s.

Dunnville had its share of moneyed individuals as the homes along
Alder and Broad Street will indicate. Nicknamed the Monarch Mansions,
they include the 1860s-era MacDonald Mansion built in the French Second

Dunnville's main street remains busy and boasts many heritage buildings.

Empire style for a dry goods merchant while the Lalor house at Church and Alder is one the town's finest. Built in 1906 for Frances Ramsey Lalor, owner of the two largest dry goods outlets in Dunnville, it is known today as the Lalor Estate Inn, a popular bed and breakfast. Lalor went on to own an apple evaporator, said by some to be North America's largest, and the Monarch Knitting Mills. Lalor also served as Haldimand County's federal member of parliament from 1904 until 1921.

On Main Street, west of Queen, a riverside park stretches along the banks of the Grand, adjacent to it the 1870 Braund house. A new bridge connects Dunnville with Byng, now a growing suburb of Dunnville.

Stromness

Despite a strategic location, Stromness never grew beyond a hotel and handful of homes; a stopover village for crew and passengers travelling the Welland Canal's feeder canal, and transferring either to lake vessels or to the Grand River Canal. Its post office was established in 1860. There was a mill in the village, although its chief business was boat-building.

Here, at the former site of the turning basin of the Welland Feeder canal, a wide, weedy meadow marks the junction of the main feeder canal, which which struck northeast to the Welland Canal and southwest to Lock Number 27, while the channel led northwest to the Grand River at the Dunnville dam. The feeder canal today remains visible only as weedy, water-filled ditch. The link to the Grand River Canal follows Haldimand Road 3, but remains scarcely visible for the first stretch toward Dunnville. It eventually opens into a water-filled channel, with the one-time towpath still visible on the far bank.

In Stromness, the old hotel, now a residence, still stands in the village overlooking the site of the turning basin, while newer homes mingle with the handful of early houses. Stromness lies seven kilometres southeast of Dunnville.

7
THE MIDDLE PORTS

Port Dover ~ Port Rowan ~ Port Burwell ~ Port Stanley

B etween the Grand River and the bustling port of Port Stanley, a series of small rivers and creeks carved deep notches into Lake Erie's shore cliffs, creating protected harbours large enough to shelter many of the early lake boats. Each developed a sizable fishing fleet and attracted the railways to locate termini there as well. While retaining their roles as commercial centres for the hinterland around them, over the years they have also attracted growing numbers of tourists. Many are drawn to the beaches, as at Port Dover and Port Burwell, others to nearby historical and natural features, as at Port Rowan.

Port Dover

Of Lake Erie's four "middle ports," Port Dover is arguably the most scenic. On the east side of the harbour a high bluff overlooks the Lynn River and the harbour into which it flows. On the west side, a line of cliffs looks down upon the wide and popular sand beach.

Port Dover's history also precedes that of many of its neighbouring ports. It was here in 1669 that Dollier and Galinée erected the buildings of the lake's first European wintering site. More than a century would pass, however, before another cabin would be built. These were located not in the harbour, but at a water power site on the Lynn River about two kilometres to the north. Known as Dover Mills, the little settlement consisted of the badly needed sawmill for the growing pioneer settlements and for a developing export trade, as well.

But disaster struck during the War of 1812. In 1814, a force led by Lieutenant-Colonel James Campbell landed in the harbour and set about burning the mill and all the cabins, save one, whose occupant had provided the weary Yankee militia with some bread.

In 1835, Israel Powell, a new settler, assembled a block of land at the mouth of the river and laid out what would become the townsite for Port Dover. But growth remained slow. Eventually, with the opening of a plank road to Hamilton in 1843, the little harbour began to grow. A saw and gristmill were built on Patterson Creek, and the town could count a population of four hundred.

Initially, few fishing boats bobbed along the river, catching blue pickerel and trout for the local population. But it was with the arrival of not just one, but ultimately three rail lines that Port Dover would boom.

The first rail link from Hamilton to Port Dover was proposed as early as 1835 with the chartering of the Hamilton and Port Dover Railway (H&PD). Nearly forty years would pass, however, before the first rails reached town, and those were from a different line entirely. In 1872, the tracks of the Port Dover and Lake Huron Railway (PD&LH) reached the lakeshore connecting the harbour with Simcoe, Woodstock, and Stratford. Being the first to arrive, the PD&LH Railway had the choice of the best site on the shore, and built on the flat west bank, their station, engine house, and sidings.

Five years later, the Hamilton and Northwestern Railway (H&NW), which had assumed the charter of the H&PD, extended its tracks from their existing junction at Jarvis along the narrower east shore of the Lynn River and into Port Dover. The railway added its station on the east bank of the river, just north of today's bridge.

Eventually, the two railways agreed to share the building of grain elevators on the harbour; and the H&NW was allowed to build a bridge across the river. By 1881, the Grand Trunk Railway had acquired both lines in any event, and removed its east bank station. Seven years later, the old west bank station burned, with arson suspected, and the GT replaced it with a larger and more elaborate station, along with their turntable and engine house.

In 1917, yet another railway entered town, that of the Lake Erie and Northern (LE&N). Owned by the Canadian Pacific Railway, this electric interurban line connected Port Dover with Simcoe, Waterford, and Brantford. Until 1947, it too used the station that was at that time owned by Canadian National, situated at the corner of Harbour and Main Streets. In 1947, the LE&N moved out the CN station and into its own structure between Nelson and Chapman Streets.

Shortly after the port became a bustling rail terminal, on August 17, 1895, Port Dover entered yet another new transportation age — that of the cross-lake railcar ferries. On that rainy summer day, the *Shenango 1* steamed slowly into the harbour, carrying from the port of Conneaut, Ohio, a load of coal for the steelworks in Hamilton. The ship was also capable of carrying tourists and could boast cabins and twenty staterooms, as well as parlours and a dining room.

But Port Dover's harbour proved too shallow and the *Shenango* often sailed with little or no southbound cargo. After just six years, the car ferry steamed out of Port Dover for the last time. In response, the town council lobbied hard for the federal government to make substantial improvements to the harbour. In 1906, the federal government took back control of the harbour and began to make the badly needed improvements. But even that failed to encourage the return of the coal boats. Despite the demise of the cross-lake ferries, Port Dover continued to ship grain and lumber on more than a dozen schooners. Fishing was also developing, especially with the invention of the enclosed fishing boat, and, by the 1960s, Port Dover could boast of having the world's largest freshwater fishing fleet.

Ontario Archives, S 18150.

The car ferries Shenango 1 *and* 2 *lie at the Port Dover dock.*

Meanwhile, the wide, sandy beach at Port Dover was beginning to attract tourists, many of whom travelled down on the LE&N radial streetcars. Hotels were added, such as the Orchard Beach Hotel and the Erie Hotel. The popular Norfolk House on the main street, however, had been around since at least the 1830s.

After the Second World War ended, Port Dover's rail days were winding down, as well. In 1947, the last of the LE&N streetcars left town and CN's last passenger train puffed away in 1957. In 1988, the last of the rail lines, that from Simcoe, was finally removed.

But two relics remain from Port Dover's heady train times. The handsome GT station was turned sideways and became a car wash before being moved a few blocks farther where it has become a gift store. The LE&N station, built in the flat-roofed international style popular with the Canadian Pacific after the war, was turned over to the town in 1972 and is now a municipal storage facility.

While much of its Lake Erie fleet has moved west, Port Dover remains home to a couple of dozen fishing boats.

Once the railway yards by the harbour were gone, tourism began to grow. Summer restaurants and gift shops popped up. The old Erie Hotel was removed in 1952 by Harold and Marjorie Schneider, who had bought the building six years earlier, and the new Erie Beach Hotel was erected in its place. Its Cove Room dining room is widely renowned for its salad bar and, in particular, its fresh yellow perch.

Bikers, too, discovered the place and every time there is a Friday the 13th, the Harleys rumble into town by the thousands. The tradition began on Friday, November 13, 1981, when about two-dozen local biking enthusiasts got together in a local pub and decided that every time there was a similar date, they would renew their gathering. The event quickly grew into a major motorcycle rally and has become as widely known as the bike rallies in Sturgis, South Dakota, and Daytona, Florida.

Several of the early fishing structures have been converted into tourist draws. The popular museum occupies what began as a net shanty for commercial fishermen to store and dry their nets. Today's visitors can learn the stories

One-time net sheds now house the Port Dover Harbour Museum.

of the many shipwrecks that lie beneath the waters of the lake. The Sandal-maker gift shop occupies a one-time net shed. The town hall, with its iconic clock tower, has become a well-respected summertime theatre, known as the Lighthouse Theatre.

While charter boats now line the west side of the harbour, the fishing fleet has moved into new facilities on the east side of the harbour. The pier extends well into the lake and is lined with strollers and fisher-folks trying to land din-ner. At the base of the pier, a $100,000 memorial to the fishermen of Port Dover was unveiled in the year 2000. Four metres in height, the bronze-and-granite sculpture commemorates those who lost their lives while fishing for their living. At the end of the pier, the iconic Port Dover lighthouse guides vessels into the port. The tapering steel-covered tower replaced the first such navigational aide, which was built in 1846. Boaters require a second light, located on the opposite shore, which they can then line up in order to safely enter the harbour.

In 2003, Port Dover's residents awoke to learn of a proposal for a new era in their maritime story, a "fast ferry" that would link their community with Erie, Pennsylvania, on the south shore. The study, carried out jointly between the County of Norfolk and the Erie Western Pennsylvania Port Authority, esti-mated that the 250-passenger and 46-car ferry would lure up to 750,000 rid-ers a year from the numbing line-ups and the excessive security checks at the cross-border bridges. The cost to prepare the harbour facilities would run up to $28 million. Despite letters of support from various politicians, the idea stalled when the Toronto-to-Rochester fast ferry service sank due to low ridership.

An earlier, albeit more modest, proposal suffered a similar fate. In 1927, the Port Dover Cemetery Board decided to erect and promote a mausoleum a short distance to the west of the town. Built of concrete, the structure pre-sented a facade of four Doric columns. Crypts were offered for sale for $225 to $275. "No matter how inclement the weather," the ad went, "the entrance halls of our mausoleum present a beautiful chapel." But with the Depression, and the cost, the mausoleum remained unused, and today still stands on the north side of Highway 3, an overgrown and puzzling structure to many.

But even the port's very beginnings are not forgotten. High on Brant Hill, a granite cross marks the site of the landing of the two adventurous priests, while their wintering site on Donjon Avenue is marked with a stone cairn. Inside a small, fenced enclosure are the earthworks marking that long-ago cabin where Port Dover began.

Port Rowan

Of Lake Erie's "middle" ports, Port Rowan may just be able to offer the most interesting viewpoint. From the hilltop park at the south end of the main street, the view extends over Long Point Bay to the long, low point of land that is Long Point, one of Ontario's only three UNESCO World Biosphere Reserves. But the view also reveals Long Point Bay, and the harbour, which a busy fishing fleet once called home.

Port Rowan has attracted fishermen since the first aboriginal populations entered the area. Indeed, the waters of the bay have often been called Lake Erie's fish nursery. While the fishing industry was never especially active on shore, fishing tugs from along the coast would lay their seine or hoop nets in the bay's shallow waters, hoping for a haul of whitefish, herring, or pickerel. But the fishery has had to face many challenges from invasive species, such as smelt and zebra mussels, and from pollution caused by farm runoff.

Equally important to Port Rowan's growth was what lay not just off the shore, but in back of it, as well. As with most of the Erie shore, the lands back of Port Rowan abounded in prized stands of pine and oak, commodities in high demand for both shipbuilding and masts. As a result, several mills were built on the little creeks, which flowed toward the lake. Austin Dedrick, an early arrival, built the town's first, a short distance east of the hill. But it would the next mill that would bring the village into prominence, not just then, but even today.

In 1796, John Backhouse arrived in Port Rowan and was determined to build a combined saw and gristmill about four kilometres north on the banks of Spring Creek. A year later he received his permission and he put up a three-storey mill with a flume and overshot wheel. As with most gristmills, the miller would keep a portion of the grain, which he ground for the farmer, and Backhouse kept one-tenth.

During the scorched-earth policy of the invading American militia during the War of 1812, all mills along the Erie shore as far as the Grand River were burned to the ground. All, that is, except the mill belonging to John Backhouse, and Tisdale's mill in Vittoria. Speculation has it that he was related to key people still living in the United States. If that wasn't fortuitous enough, the mill has escaped that fate ever since. While it was commonplace for mills, especially those constructed of wood, to burn, this mill has survived. Now renamed the "Backus" mill, it still grinds out flour, still using its overshot water wheel, but today it is preserved in the Backus Heritage Conservation Education Centre. Here, in the midst of a rich Carolinian forest, it shares the grounds with several other heritage buildings, moved in from threatened locations.

In its early years, the site went through a variety of name changes. Originally named John Cartwright's Landing, after the area's first settler, it became Wolven's, after Jeremiah Wolven. Within a few years it gained still another new name, Dutcher's Corners, after local landowner, John Duitcher. Then, in 1825, after a village plot was laid out, it acquired the name it still carries, that of Colonel William Rowan, who was secretary to Sir John Colborne, Upper Canada's lieutenant governor from 1828 until 1836.

The little port did not grow quickly. By 1816, it could count no more than a handful of merchants and craftsmen. By 1845, it remained below its potential as was described by W.H. Smith in his 1865 *Canadian Gazeteer*. He noted that it was: "a village of considerable importance laid out in 1825, but by 1845 contained only 1 store, shops and 16 houses." As Smith observed, its potential lay in its resources. "In the rear of this place are large lumber districts and from them immense quantities are annually shipped. The total exports as of June 30, 1865 including lumber and grain amounted to almost $1/4 million." A dockside building housed furs and buffalo skins from the western plains awaiting the fur merchants from New York.[1]

By 1850, it was starting to grow and had doubled its population. Pine logs and lumber exceeded 4 million metres in 1849. By this time its streets offered a pair of general stores, three hotels, as well as carriage makers and a range of craftsmen. By 1857, its population had climbed to 450. In fact, Port Rowan was getting so busy that it became necessary to start building ships on nearby Dedrick Creek, a short distance west from the harbour. The first was likely the *Garibaldi*, built by Woodward and Killmaster in 1863. It was followed by others, such as the *A.H. Jenny*, which measured sixty metres long and carried lumber and grain between Buffalo, Rondeau, and Cleveland.

David Foster, another local shipbuilder, began turning out boats from his shipyard around the same time, but he spread his shipbuilding operations to other early ports, as well, including Port Burwell, Port Ryerse, and Port Dover.

Port Rowan became a hive of small industry. Near the dock stood a steam sawmill and gristmill. A brickyard turned out bricks from 1909 until the 1930s, while the evaporator at the Simcoe Canning Company processed up to 40,000 bushels of dried apples a year.

But with road travel being cumbersome, and water travel being seasonal and hazardous, the town began to lobby for a rail line. Eventually, in 1886, the first train of what was called the South Norfolk Railway, puffed into town. A mixed passenger and freight train, it was dubbed "The Daily Effort" by locals. Two trains ran between Port Rowan and Simcoe each day. From Simcoe, freight could carry on to Hamilton. Besides Simcoe and Port Rowan, stations were located at Vittoria and St. Williams. The end of the railway era began in 1957 when the mail contract was cancelled, ending passenger service at the same time. Freight service struggled on until 1965, but it remained a losing proposition for the CNR, and, despite objections from the town, the Board of Transportation Commissioners approved the CNR's request for abandonment.

The end of the railway did not spell doom for Port Rowan. Roads were improved, and the town continued to grow. Today it has become a jumping-off point for nature enthusiasts and vacationers heading for Long Point. Before leaving for that destination, they can pause in a park overlooking the harbour and ponder a large, interpretative sign that describes the story of the Long Point Biosphere Reserve stretching before them to the distant horizon. At the east end of town, an unmarked pullover allows an unobstructed view of the same feature.

While fishing boats no longer bob in the harbour, the boathouses now provide shelter for pleasure craft. A dockside restaurant occupies what was once a fish-processing plant, while a small picnic park allows visitors to relax and watch the coming and going of the "fleet." Above the hill that overlooks the bay, the main street is busy and well maintained, although few buildings have survived from its early years.

Port Rowan lies on Norfolk County Road 59, about eighty kilometres southwest of Brantford.

Port Burwell

It is hard to believe that the bucolic little village of Port Burwell was once one of Lake Erie's most industrialized ports. Grassy meadows and weedy shorelines are all that remain of the rail yards, the shipyards, and the car ferry docks that drove the town's economic engines. It is no surprise that its name honours the man who first surveyed the town and then started up the harbour company that caused the port to boom.

Once alive with fishing boats, Port Rowan's harbour is now home to pleasure craft and sports-fishing boats.

In 1810, Colonel Mahlon Burwell, surveyor for Thomas Talbot, laid out the lots of the surrounding township of Malahide (named appropriately after Talbot's ancestral castle in Ireland). Burwell's next job was to extend the Talbot Road west toward Amherstburg on the Detroit River. In 1818, he surveyed yet another township, Bayham, and was given 480 hectares of land as a reward for his earlier survey work for Thomas Talbot. Finally, in 1830, he laid out what would become the village that would take his name. But he wasn't done yet, for, in order to ensure his town would prosper, he then deeded two-and-a-half hectares to the Port Burwell Harbour Company to develop the mouth of the creek into a navigable harbour from which lumber and farm products could be exported. In 1833, the Harbour company began to dredge the river mouth and erected wharves.

But it was not just the presence of the protected estuary of Big Otter Creek that launched Port Burwell's growth; it was the rich Carolinian forests, thick with oak trees that proved to be one of the port's earliest exports. During the heyday of lumbering, more than twenty-nine sawmills were operating in the area, shipping up to four hundred shiploads of staves and planks every year. Pine, too, was in high demand for ships' masts, destined primarily for the Royal Navy, which paid five dollars per foot of lumber. Much lumber was also exported to the United States to supply its burgeoning construction industry.

But inland connections were important, too, and in 1851 a plank road was opened between Ingersoll and the growing port. Stagecoaches rattled daily between the two towns, stopping at any of the sixteen stage coach taverns that lined the route. In that same year, the port saw the arrival of its first steamer. The port then began what is likely its least known industrial stage, the busy shipbuilding period. Thanks again to the vast lumber resources, the town soon claimed three shipyards. Production peaked during the 1860s and 1870s, when the shipyards turned out schooners large enough to fill the locks of the Welland Canal. Among the largest were the *Lady Dufferin* at 322 tonnes, the *Lady Hamilton* at 290, while the *Edward Blake* weighed in at 297 tonnes, and the *Erie Belle* at 289.

The federal government continued to make improvements to the growing harbour and eventually a rubblestone breakwater extended more than one thousand metres into the lake. In 1844, a tall wooden lighthouse was built on a bank overlooking the river near the end of the main street, an icon which would later become the symbol of the town.

Shipbuilding here dates back to 1820, with the launch of the first tug, the *Royal Tar,* a small vessel of just 36 tonnes. Since then, between 1821 and 1918, more than fifty schooners were launched from Port Burwell. The industry resumed in the 1940s and lasted until the 1980s with the Hurley Boating Building yard. Here, Ralph Hurley, founder of the company, built more than a half-dozen tugs, the last being a pleasure craft called the *Aurora Borealis II.*

In 1895, the Lake Erie and Tillsonburg Railway laid its tracks into the town, locating its station, yards, and turntable on the flat floodplain of the river's east bank. As far back as 1875, plans were being pushed for what was then called the Tillsonburg, Lake Erie and Pacific Railway. (How they proposed reaching the Pacific from a line that went to Lake Erie is not recorded.) In 1906, the CPR added the line to its own vast network and began running car ferries to Ashtabula, Ohio. Most of the trade was one-way, however, with railcars carrying coal for the CPR making their way north, while the only export out of the port was lumber and soon that dwindled (although it was rumoured that whisky was a common cargo during the American days of prohibition).

The most dominant structure on Port Burwell's otherwise modest main street is this wooden lighthouse.

Following a rebound during the war years, the trans-lake shipments sputtered on until 1958 when the car ferry, the *Ashtabula*, struck the steamer, *Ben Moreel*, in Ashtabula Harbour. However, business did not justify repairing the boat and the mighty vessel was scrapped.

As with nearly all of Lake Erie's ports, fishing became a mainstay, especially following the arrival of the railway. Fish could be packaged and shipped to markets on the trains, rather than being sold locally. In the early 1950s, Port

Burwell harbour was home to twenty-one fishing tugs. A decade later, after the railway closed, there were only four.

With its wide, sandy beaches, Port Burwell began to appeal to vacationers, as well. Those travelling by rail would make for Jubilee Park at the foot of the hill on the west bank of the river to ride the merry-go-round, soak in the bathhouses, or dance the night away in the casino. After the First World War, a second park, Memorial Park, was established on the east bank with a campground, gardens, and a zoo.

Port Burwell is quiet now, the tracks and the amusement parks but a memory. Few buildings remain to celebrate the port's heritage on the main street, although a few early buildings lie on its back streets. Jubilee Park is now a local beach, while Memorial Park has morphed into Iroquois Beach Provincial Park. The riverbanks lie overgrown with no evidence of the railway or the shipyards. Three fishing boats still tie up and sell fish from an outlet on the west bank of the river.

But the most prominent feature of the town, and one of the more interesting structures of the Lake Erie shore, is the tall, wooden lighthouse that still

A small fishery still occupies Port Burwell's harbour.

commands the harbour from its location at the foot of the main street. Built in 1840, the lighthouse remains one of the oldest in Canada. Rising twenty metres above the ground and sixty metres above the lake level, the light served as the only beacon of safe haven along the cliff-lined shore for many kilometres in either direction. While the light's first keeper was Thomas Bellairs, beginning with Alexander Sutherland, the Sutherland family members served as keepers for a full century from 1852 to 1952.

In 1963, the lights finally dimmed for good. Two years later it became a national historic site, and in 1983 was opened to the public. During the next four years, local craftsmen, using similar tools to those used on the first lighthouse, replaced beams and the staircase. Visitors can now safely climb to the top to see the lens that so faithfully served sailors making their way along the lake's perilous shores. Nearby, the Port Burwell Marine Museum depicts the maritime history of the area and houses one the largest collections of lighthouse lenses on the Great Lakes. The local library is named after the port's most famous luminary, Fred Bodsworth, author of many nature books and the best selling title *Last of the Curlews*, which has sold more than three million copies.

Port Burwell lies at the end of Elgin Road 79, twenty-five kilometres south of Tillsonburg.

Port Stanley

Over the years, nothing has seemed to slow Port Stanley down. From its earliest days as a coal port, railway terminal, and later amusement park, it still attracts tourists, ships, and rail buffs.

The harbour where Kettle Creek enters Lake Erie had interested the area's leading colonizer, Thomas Talbot, as early as 1801. Four years later, he awarded a land grant on the site to his friend Colonel John Bostwick. It would be another thirteen years, however, before Bostwick, who had by then become the sheriff of London District, would arrive to take up his land. In 1823, Talbot decided to name the port after another of his friends, Baron Edward George Stanley, 14th Earl of Derby, whose son, Frederick Arthur Stanley, would become Canada's governor general and donate to the hockey world the elusive (to certain teams) trophy, which still bears his name.

Following the opening of a rough wagon road to London in 1822, Port Stanley began to grow as a port through which grain and lumber would flow.

After the rebellion of 1837, the military planked and straightened the trail, making the community more accessible. However, in 1851, the fledgling village suffered a setback when the seat for the newly created County of Elgin went to St. Thomas instead of the port.

But grand days were in the offing. In 1853, shortly after the Great Western Railway had reached London, work began on a line that would link that growing industrial centre with the port. Three years later, trains began rolling into town. As a result, the federal government began major improvements to the harbour, spending over £200,000 to extend and deepen it.

Industry came quickly, as well. Shipbuilding soon became an important industry in the town. In fact, even before the trains began to arrive, the port enjoyed an active marine service with steamers like the *Telegraph* and schooners like the *Union* linking the town with Cleveland, Ohio. A veritable fleet ran between Port Stanley and Buffalo, while cruise ships like the *Joe Milton* were instrumental in the town's early popularity as a tourist destination.

By 1865, tourists from places like London were literally riding the rooftops of the London and Port Stanley trains. The Fraser House opened on a height of land known as Picnic Hill in 1871, providing easy access to the beaches below by a steam-powered incline railway that replaced the original steep

Port Stanley's amusement park is seen from the top of Picnic Hill.

Elgin County Archives, Elgin County Photo Collection, P60.

set of stairs. The hotel offered sixty-two rooms, most with shared bath, and a two-hundred-seat dining hall. From the hill, the braver visitors could climb a thirty-metre observation tower, which had seven viewing levels. Around the foot of the tower, a small amusement park was taking shape with swings and a hand operated merry-go-round.

As inhibitions were shed, swimming became more popular and the beach began its long evolution into one of the lake's more popular attractions. In 1907, a group of local investors formed the Port Stanley Amusement Company and began to develop the beach itself, changing the name of the Fraser House to the Invererie, where they added lawn bowling, a roller rink, and dance hall.

The City of London took over the operation of the railway in 1913, and, following the First World War, made still more improvements to the park. In the 1930s, the grounds contained a ferris wheel, two merry-go-rounds, a bowling alley, two theatres, and thirty refreshment stands and amusement booths. The stationary steam engine which had until then powered the incline railway was replaced with an electric motor. But with the beach attracting ever more day visitors, the Invererie stood empty and was demolished in 1919.

Perhaps the most famous addition was that of the Pavilion in 1926. It would later gain continent wide fame as the "Stork Club." Here, in a

The Port Stanley dance pavilion was one of Ontario's most popular; hosting internationally renowned dance bands such as that of Guy Lombardo.

two-thousand-square-metre ballroom, dancers would swing and sway to the sounds of Vince Lopez, Emerson Gill, and later, Guy Lombardo. Admission to the Pavilion was fifteen cents with five cents charged for each dance. After each dance finished, bouncers used ropes to clear the dance floor, preventing those who lingered from getting a free dance. In the 1950s, the dance floor area was reduced so that tables and chairs could be added. The name changed to the Stork Club, a name which resonates up to today. The story of the Stork Club reached its zenith when, on September 6, 1950, more than 7,000 fans flocked to see Guy Lombardo and His Royal Canadians. At its peak, Port Stanley Beach could claim bathhouses, dance clubs, a roller coaster, ferris wheel, and two carousels along with swimming pools, theatres, and no fewer than thirty concessions.

The trains of the L&PS hauled not only tourists but freight, as well. By 1903, the railway belonged to the American-owned Père Marquette Railroad, which also operated coal boats across the lake. These shipments operated sporadically even after 1913, when the L&PS was sold to London, and electrified. Gradually, profits decreased to a point in 1932 when the car ferries were no longer worth operating and the service ended.

As with many such places around Ontario, the arrival of the car craze after the Second World War made operating the train line less and less worthwhile. In 1957, passenger service ceased and by 1982, the section between the port and St. Thomas was abandoned entirely. Most Londoners owned cars and began to find the waters of Lake Huron more appealing than those of Lake Erie, which were becoming increasingly polluted by agricultural runoff and by chemical industries on the American side. By 1946, the beach was down to only a pair of rides and a handful of games and concessions. The amusement park saw fewer and fewer revellers and one by one the attractions closed. The Incline Railway carried its last passengers in 1966. The last of the buildings to go was the Stork Club, which, despite being refurbished in 1973, burned in 1979.

Much has changed in Port Stanley, most of it for the better. State and provincial regulations have greatly reduced pollution levels in the lake. In 1983, trains began running into Port Stanley again. The previous year, a group of London and St. Thomas businessmen had bought the old line and began to refurbish the deteriorating roadbed. Renamed the Port Stanley Terminal Railway, the trains now haul tourists who are there to experience the nostalgia of rail travel as it used to be. In 1988, the line was reopened right into St. Thomas.

The iconic incline railway cars from Port Stanley beach rest now in the Elgin County Railway Museum at St. Thomas.

The line's only surviving stations were the flag station at Union (North America's smallest "Union" station), and the larger station in Port Stanley itself, which now houses a gift shop and ticket office. The odd-looking little cars from the incline railway are still around and now reside at the Elgin County Railway Museum at St. Thomas.

The beach area, too, has undergone a facelift. New boardwalks and change rooms have replaced the old, and a larger parking lot can be filled on a warm summer weekend. The usual condos have crowded into the western end of the former park. Many of the early restaurants and small hotels can yet be found along William Street, which leads to the beach, but the only one of the park's names to remain is that of Mackie's snack bar. Although the building is new, there has been a Mackie's at Stanley Park since 1913.

The port area itself has changed, as well. While fishing boats can still be seen in the harbour, the shoreline now offers a landscaped parkette, especially by the 1937 King George VI lift bridge (the oldest of its kind in Ontario), while inns and bed and breakfasts offer portside accommodations, among them the historic Kettle Creek Inn and the newer Inn on the Harbour. On Main Street, which lines the east side of the harbour, lies a maritime legacy of former fishing buildings, net sheds, and even a small concrete hut used to dry

With landscaping improvements, Port Stanley's harbourfront has become one of Lake Erie's most attractive.

early wooden fishing floats. Many of these buildings now offer silk scarves, antiques, crafts, and other gifts, as well as fresh fish.

The 140-seat Port Stanley Festival Theatre has moved into the Village Hall, Port Stanley's former town hall, while a new library houses many of the stories of this active and historic Lake Erie port.

Port Stanley lies at the end of County Road 4, about a dozen kilometres south of St. Thomas.

8

THE WEST END

Erieau ~ Wheatley ~ Leamington ~ Kingsville

W est of Port Stanley, no tributaries of any significance flow into Lake Erie. Thanks to an ancient post-glacial beach ridge, all streams flow north into the Thames River. This left few rivermouth harbours available to accommodate shipping. Along this stretch only the bay enclosed by Point aux Pins offered any sizable opportunity for a harbour, while a small creek at Wheatley allowed for the creation of what is today the lake's busiest fishing harbour.

Erieau

While Point aux Pins was noted by the travelling priests, Daillon and Galinée, they had no chance to comment on the protective bay behind it. Not until the governor of Upper Canada, John Graves Simcoe, began to investigate the military potential of Lake Erie, did he realize the potential of the bay as protected harbour. It had been named Rondeau, derived from "Ronde Eau," due to the shape of the bay. Simcoe ordered his surveyors to open a road that would link the navigable Thames River with Rondeau Bay, where he set aside a military reserve. At the shoreline he laid out a townsite for which he envisioned an eventual county seat.

But Simcoe's plans remained dormant. When the Rebellion of 1837 exposed the inadequacy of Ontario's defences, the government revisited many such early military opportunities. That concern, along with the recommendations in the Durham Report[1] on local government, launched a major program of public works across the colony. When a schooner, the *Windsor*, sank in a vicious squall off the point, the government realized that the overlooked Rondeau Bay needed a second look and should be opened up as a harbour.

In 1844, the authorities spent £75,000 (CAD$135,000) to cut a channel through the sandbar that enclosed the west end of the bay. To guide the ships through the new cut, they erected a lighthouse and in 1845, Rondeau Harbour had become a port of entry.

Still, despite its newfound accessibility, for the most part, Rondeau Harbour remained little used. The only activity was from a wharf at Raglan at the terminus of the road from the Thames, where small quantities of lumber were exported.

The extensive community today known as Erieau, located beside the piers in the sandbar, began with the arrival of the Erie and Huron Railway in 1894. By combining "Lake Erie" with "Ronde Eau," the railway came up with "Erieau." Originally, the line was to run from Shrewsbury to Sarnia, where the railway company owned the piers. But because the waters at the Shrewsbury harbour remained shallow, the railway deliberated instead locating its Lake Erie terminus near the channel that the government had cut through the western sandbar. An impediment, however, still remained in an extensive area of marsh lying between the sandbar and the mainland.

Finally, in 1889, the railway decided on Erieau. As the *Chatham Planet* noted: "The main line has been extended along the lake beach to the Rondeau piers (Erieau) which, during the season of navigation will be a port of call for a line of steamers from across the lake … Besides, it will prove a great convenience to the numerous families who, during the summer, reside in lake side cottages." In 1892, the piers were rebuilt and the next year the passenger ship, the *Byron Trerice*, began running between Cleveland and Erieau.

Daily trains between Chatham and Erieau turned the port into a busy summer colony. Cottages and summer homes were built along the sandbar along which the tracks ran, and a popular hotel, the Bungalow Hotel, began operation. The Chatham newspaper glowingly reported the hotel as "a fine wooden structure of modern architecture and fitted with up-to-date requirements." The hotel could accommodate more than two hundred guests. Although liquor was forbidden, the twice-weekly dances attracted trainloads of patrons from Chatham. A smaller hotel, the Lakeview, was soon added. The trains made three stops as they traversed the sandbar, Jubilee, Centreville, and Crafords.

Tourists arriving by train walk from the station to the Bungalow Hotel.

But Erieau had an industrial raison d'être as well. Like other railway ports, Erieau became important in the shipping of coal. In 1899, the Lake Erie and Detroit River Railway, which had by then acquired the Erie and Huron, added a terminus at Erieau, in addition to those at Port Stanley and Port Dover. However, because the harbour at Port Dover was proving inadequate, and because the railway had failed to complete a promised link from Windsor to Port Stanley, Erieau became the railway's major coal importation terminus. Ships like the *Marquette* and *Bessemer I* and *II*, and the *Shenango* carried coal between Conneaut or Toledo and Erieau.

After the Père Marquette acquired the rail line, the coal company launched one of the largest coal vessels to ply Lake Erie. Known as the *Alexander Leslie*, the mighty carrier measured 122 metres by 16 metres and could carry 5,500 tonnes of coal. Unlike the car ferries, which ran out of Port Burwell and Port Stanley, this vessel carried no railcars. Despite the attraction of the summer resort, the coal terminal became Erieau's most prominent feature. With a coal hoist that cost $100,000, the coal storage area measured 190 metres by 80 metres and could accommodate 65,000 tonnes of anthracite coal.

With the growing popularity of the car, and the building of a road along the edge of the marsh, passenger service on the trains dwindled and the last passenger train ran to Erieau in 1932. The station lingered on, derelict, until

Erieau's fishing fleet awaits the call to head out into the lake.

1954, when it was finally demolished. While the Bungalow Hotel burned in 1912, the Lakeview has managed to survive and the building still stands.

The coal business, too, was doomed as railways were quickly switching to diesel power. In 1964, the *Alexander Leslie* departed Erieau for the last time and, in 1972, the tracks to the coal docks were lifted.

Still, Erieau remains a popular summer destination. A landscaped boulevard now occupies the old railway right-of-way. More modern year-round homes line the beach, although many summer cottages still crowd the laneways. Sports fishermen now cast their lines into what was the large slip into which the *Alexander Leslie* and her predecessors would glide, while a newer harbour now is home to a growing fleet of fishing boats. The piers, however, are empty and overgrown, while a solitary caboose in Memorial Park by the beach is the only evidence that Erieau was once one of western Lake Erie's busiest coal terminals.

Erieau sits at the end of Elgin Road 12 about forty kilometres south of Chatham.

Wheatley

There have always been two Wheatleys. There was the Talbot Road village, and that which developed around the mouth of Muddy Creek, three kilometres away on the shore of Lake Erie. Completed in 1818, the Talbot Road in this area followed an early Indian trail along one of the lake's many postglacial beach ridges. Because the lake was easier to travel than the rugged Talbot Road, the earliest families settled closer to the shore. To keep their homes above the many inundations of the lake, they constructed them on small stilts, earning their fledgling community the name "Pegtown."

Interest in developing a harbour surfaced early. In 1817, Caleb Coatsworth had sent off a petition to the commissioner of Crown lands, advising that he intended on building a dock on the shore of Lake Erie in front of Lot 200, Talbot Road, as there was no nearby dock for shipping timber, lumber staves, cordwood, or produce. It had also been Coatsworth's dream to realize a shipping canal that would link Lake Erie from this point with Lake St. Clair. Although the government showed no interest in such an undertaking. Coatsworth went ahead with his dock, which later became known more simply as Coatsworth's Dock, which was located two kilometres from the mouth of Muddy Creek. In the 1870s, the village post office, located on the Talbot Road east of where Wheatley was developing, adopted the name "Romney," after an early port in England.

One of the first settlers to brave the Talbot Road was Richard Wheatley, who took up his parcel of land in 1832. After he died shortly before 1864, Wheatley's son-in-law, William Buchanan, convinced the post office to name the village after Wheatley to honour the bravery of the area's first pioneer.

Because of its location on the Talbot Road, Wheatley was developing as an important stagecoach stop. By 1862, teams of horses would trot to a halt before the hotels of Jacob Julian or J.R. Thompson. Nearby, the travellers could shop at Thomas Dales's general store, the village's first. A few years later, census takers counted 150 residents. The first church was built in 1866 and others followed soon after. Soon the village was home to a full range of craftsmen and industries including a shoemaker, carpenter, wagon factory, and a sawmill, as well as butchers, bakers, and blacksmiths.

In 1857, the MacLean family began the area's first fish operation, marking the beginning of an industry that has led the community to its present prominence as the lake's leading fishery. A short distance east of the mouth of the sluggish Muddy Creek, MacLean built a wooden dock along with grain storage. Such an opportunity to ship their produce encouraged farmers to increase their production. Many also put out nets and poles of their own, as Wheatley's early fishing techniques were primarily for local consumption.

The next growth spurt followed the arrival of the Lake Erie Essex and Detroit River (LE&D) Railway in 1891. Shipping no longer needed to depend upon the seasonal variations of the lake, and many fishermen placed their catch on the station's wooden platform. The railway also encouraged the growth of the fishery. At first, most fishermen used pound nets. But then with the building of larger enclosed tugs, fish could be hauled directly on board and placed in ice-filled boxes.

Still, Wheatley lacked any real harbour. Finally, in 1912, the government built new piers to replace the old structures that had belonged to the dozen or so family fishing operations; including the Gettys, the Omsteads,

The much-enlarged harbour at Wheatley today houses the largest fishing fleet on the Great Lakes.

and the MacLeans. In 1940, the E. Omstead company fishery added Wheatley's first freezing equipment, allowing fish to be ice-packed as soon they arrived at the dock.

The rough wooden stores of the main street underwent a drastic change when, in 1890, a fire raged through the commercial district, destroying many of the original wooden buildings. Soon solid brick stores and shops rose from the ashes, many of them still in place today. Then, in 1897, a new and unexpected industry literally burst upon the scene. Gas was discovered beneath the flat soils and, by 1907, seven wells were supplying gas to homes and the village street lights as well. But the supply soon ran dry and the promising gas industry faded. However, it came roaring back to life in 1935, when gas, which had slowly been seeping from an abandoned well, blew up in the midst of one of the downtown business blocks.

Had Caleb Coatsworth still been around in 1948, he would have been pleased to see that the federal government was finally taking a major interest, to the tune of $50,000, in developing Wheatley's harbour. By 1951, the mouth of Muddy Creek had been dredged and straightened, replacing the dilapidated 1912 dock. In 1980, the creek was enlarged to accommodate sixty berths for the fishing fleet and is now classified as a federal small craft harbour. In 2006, the government was at it again, announcing more funding to help dredge the silt-infested harbour.

Today, in addition to a large dry dock and a Ministry of Natural Resources office, Wheatley's harbour, for the moment, protects the tugs of the lake's largest fishing fleet, with four fisheries offering outlet fish sales, including Omstead's fish plant offering "plenty of seafood" and MacPac, today's name for the MacLean's operations, boasting of "quality fish products since 1848." New homes have now replaced the early cabins that had made up Pegtown.

Three kilometres north, the roadside village has become a substantial town with solid brick stores at the four main corners. Handsome homes, old and new, line the streets, while what is called "Pier Road" leads to a campground and lakeside park. To the east, Wheatley Provincial Park offers camping, canoeing, and swimming, as well as trails that allow naturalists to engage in birdwatching and nature appreciation.

All evidence of the railway, however, has long vanished. Passenger service ended in 1939 and the station was removed in the 1970s. The tracks were removed soon after. Similarly, Caleb Coatsworth's dock — the place that started it all — has gone with no trace.

Gone for several decades, the Wheatley railway station was an elegant building.

Leamington

Now proudly proclaimed as the "Tomato Capital of Canada," Leamington once almost had the dubious distinction of being the "square" tomato capital of the country.

The first settler to arrive on the low shores of the lake near what is today Leamington was Alex Wilkinson, who took up his land in 1804. Being on a busy stage route, Wilkinson's Corners attracted a few hotels, one of which was built by Leonard Wigle in 1837. Growth was slow and, by 1848, the location contained just a small collection of cabins, the nearest place of any size or importance being the port at Albertville, a short distance to the west. By 1850, however, things began to look up. William Gains had added a mill and the community then adopted his name, calling itself Gainsborough. But because another community was already using the name for its post office, Gains suggested that the new post office be called Leamington after his hometown, Royal Leamington Spa in England.

In 1854, a reciprocity treaty with the United States allowed freer trade and, in 1866, the federal government responded by issuing grants to encourage the building of docks to export sand, cord wood, timber, staves, ties, and wheat. With a productive hinterland, Leamington earned three such wharfs. The opening of the Welland Canal three decades earlier had already brought regular schooner and steamboat connections to Windsor. Lumber remained Leamington's main export, with William Armstrong being the town's leading lumber merchant

The Leamington and St. Clair Railway was extended in 1887 to the wharfs from Comber, and the following year, Hiram Walker's railway, the Lake Erie and Detroit River Railway, reached Leamington, as well. A few years later, in 1908, a radial electric streetcar line connected Leamington with Kingsville and Windsor. As usual, the railways brought with them hordes of tourists anxious to enjoy the cooling lake breezes, and an area known a Seacliffe developed along the shore. The core of the town, however, remained three kilometres to the north along Talbot Road.

Long before vegetable-growing began to dominate, Leamington was the centre of Ontario's first tobacco industry when the Erie Tobacco Company was formed in 1900. In the same year, the town realized that it was surrounded by gas fields, a product that supplied the town's needs until the 1950s, when it was acquired by the Dominion Natural Gas Company. The search for oil, however, despite discoveries elsewhere on the Erie shore, proved disappointing.

Dock improvements took hold in the 1930s, with the government financing a 160-metre extension of the dock at the end of Erie Street, the town's major north-south artery. Dredging cleared out the silt and a new warehouse was added. In 1957, a 330-metre breakwater added further protection while the docks were widened and an adjustable ramp was installed for the car ferries to Pelee Island and Sandusky, Ohio. However, when the Canada Steamship Lines stopped calling in the 1960s, in favour of shipping freight to its facilities in Windsor, the docks fell silent.

That, however, would not last. With the launching of the Owen Sound Transportation Company's new car and passenger ferry, the *Jiimaan*, in 1994, tourist travel to Pelee Island grew swiftly and today reservations are needed to secure a car space on the fifty-five-car ferry. The wooden lighthouse, which guided ships safely into the Leamington harbour since 1880, has been moved a short distance from its pierside location and now rests on private property.

But Leamington doesn't promote itself as the "tomato capital" for no reason. In 1908, the town council lured the pickle company Heinz to town with an offer of a free plant that had been vacated by the Ward Tobacco Company, and a tax-free bonus. After sticking to pickles for the first few years, Heinz

A 1930s Heinz building facade has survived subsequent expansions and renovations.

began its venture into ketchup, and tomato-growing took over most of the area farms. The company expanded its plant in 1936 and again in 1957. Further enlargements took place in 1964 and 1966. With the departure of the Canada Steamship Company in 1964, Heinz switched entirely to shipping by rail. Today that has been replaced with trucks.

Much of Leamington's heritage remains today, albeit modernized. Clearly, the Heinz factory is the most visible, taking up several city blocks on Erie Street South. A giant "tomato" on Talbot Street in the downtown core houses an information booth. While most of the Heinz infrastructure dates from recent expansions, the 1930s factory still stands on the east side of the street. Leamington's industrial wealth is evident in the grand homes that line Russell Street just south of the main intersection, while its pioneer era is reflected in the still-standing 1837 Wigle tavern on Talbot St. East. While many solid stores concentrate in the core, Wharram's Jewellery, on Talbot Street West, reflects an elaborate example of commercial architecture and dates from 1908.

Leamington. A truckload of tomatoes is ready to roll.

Some visitors may be surprised to see business signs in Spanish. Since 1966, Leamington farms have hosted many of Ontario's 20,000 migrant farm workers, most arriving from Jamaica and Trinidad, but more recently many hail from Mexico. Enough Mexicans now work on Leamington area farms that the town now has its own Mexican consulate. The farm immigrant program, it is thought, dates to the efforts to produce a square tomato, one that could be easily plucked by mechanized pickers. But the oddly shaped vegetable proved tasteless, and, to save money, the growers switched instead to the use of low-paid migrant workers. The minimum wage which they earn, however, can equal ten times what they might earn in their home country. Still, efforts continue to improve working and living conditions. Thanks to these workers, the Leamington area claims to have the largest concentration of greenhouses in North America. The greenhouse operation has expanded into one of the Leamington area's most popular tourist attractions in what has become the Colasanti Tropical Gardens. In addition to the greenhouse, Colasanti's has expanded to include a restaurant, gift shop, sports store, and children's rides. Leamington's tourist trade thrives in the line of fast food outlets that line Erie Street South near the wharf, where the renovated historic Seacliffe House still stands.

The town's railway legacy was less fortunate. Both rail lines have been abandoned; those of the former LE&DR (later the Michigan Central) are nowhere to be seen. Despite efforts to save it, the elegant station was destroyed by fire in the 1990s. Portions of the tracks to the Heinz factory remain in place, and the simple wooden station which served them still stands (at least as of this writing), although now vandalized and fenced off.

Leamington is approximately fifty kilometres southeast of Windsor.

Kingsville

Kingsville's heritage has enjoyed a happier fate. Starting with the station, the stone building, designed by George Mason in the Richardsonian Romanesque style, was rescued from its dilapidated state, and now forms the focus of a newly planted arboretum. The tracks, which once lay in front, have been removed to be replaced by the Chrysler Canada Greenway, a walking and cycling corridor that links the village of Ruthven with the outskirts of Windsor.

The Richardsonian stone station in Kingsville was rescued and restored and is now a trail centre for the Chrysler Canada Greenway.

Kingsville began when James King, a settler looking for a likely property while travelling on the Talbot Road, needed to take shelter from a raging storm. Impressed by the area, he decided to stay and build a house. The town took his name, as did the house, which he built in 1855 and named Kingsholme. This unusual octagonal structure now serves as a bed and breakfast known as the Kingswood Inn.

Docks were added and a fishing industry began in 1853 when Loop and Brothers began sending their boats out in search of pickerel or bass. Lumber and grain were soon being shipped out, as well. The arrival of the Lake Erie and Detroit River Railway (LE&DR) in 1887 boosted the town's fortunes. The Ross Tobacco Company and the Conklin Lumber Company both opened large operations close to the station. The LE&DR line brought the town its first flock of tourists who headed straight for the Paradise Grove Park, a wooded gully that lined Mill Creek near the shores of the lake.

When the radial railway known as the Windsor Essex and Lakeshore Rapid Railway arrived, it brought with it the potential for more tourism. Inspired, history tells us, by the trend toward urban parks such as New York's Central Park, the town purchased eleven-and-a-quarter acres of lakeshore

Kingsville harbour is still home to a handful of fishing boats.

The photogenic stone bridge in Lakeside Park enhanced Kingsville's early appeal to tourists.

property and laid out Lakeside Park. Here, in the shady gully, the most appealing feature is a stone bridge added in the 1920s.

But aside from the park, much of Kingsville's early tourist legacy has gone. Park Street leads east from the park to the harbour where the King's Landing Hotel marks the last of the old hotels. Lakeview Avenue, farther east, was lined with upscale hotels, including the grand old Mettawas Hotel. Later replaced with a newer structure in 1914, the building sat empty and vandalized in its later years. It finally burned in 2000. Here, however, one can still find handsome homes such as that at number 229, built in 1910 by Gordon McGregor, the first general manager of the Ford Company of Canada.

The protected harbour still retains a handful of fishing boats and a fish-packing plant beside them. As with most harbours, that in Kingsville needed a lighthouse, and in 1886 a pair of wooden range lights was added, one on the shore, the other atop the hill behind it. While the rear light has been replaced by a more modern light, the original building was moved to a location near the railway station to undergo restoration to its original condition. On the hill overlooking the harbour stands the sole visible relic of the radial streetcar line, the railway's power house. Now, however, it sits vacant and overgrown.

Many of Kingsville's large houses date from the railway era as well, and they line the wide and shady Division Street south of Talbot Street. Among them, the Coda Leach house at 111, built in 1885 in the Queen Anne style, was the first in Kingsville to be declared a heritage home. The Curtis Green House at number 78 was built in 1893 by the owner of the lumber mill, while number 86 was added by A. Eastman, the vice president of the Mettawas Company, who encouraged both the building of the railway and what would be the town's grandest hotel. The oldest building in the community is believed to be a small stone house located north on Jasperson Lane, built in 1831.

The main street has retained its heritage, as well. Despite some new intrusions, the Kingsville Hotel, and a nearby block of commercial buildings all hearken to the town's boom times, and in the case of the hotel, before even that.

Kingsville is twelve kilometres west of Leamington.

9
ERIE'S GHOST COAST
The Forgotten Ports

Lowbanks ~ Selkirk ~ Nanticoke ~ Port Ryerse ~ Normandale ~ St. Williams
Troyer ~ Port Royal ~ Clear Creek ~ Houghton ~ Port Bruce ~ Jamestown
Port Talbot ~ Tyrconnell ~ Eagle ~ Port Glasgow ~ Clearville
Antrim ~ Shrewsbury ~ Union and Albertville ~ Colchester

There is much that makes Lake Erie's Canadian shoreline different from those of the other Great Lakes. It is accessible, unlike the shore of Lake Huron, where the roads run well back from the water's edge; unlike the shore of Lake Ontario, whose shoreline is massively overdeveloped; and unlike the shores of Georgian Bay, where topography has impeded easy access. Its heritage still lingers in the larger towns and villages. However, it is mostly the serenity of the forgotten little ports, mill towns, and long-ago industries that hearken the visitor to these seemingly faraway shores. The overview of the communitries that follows moves along the shoreline from east to west.

Lowbanks

As the name implies, the physical nature of the shoreline here is one of flat limestone bedrock and a low-lying hinterland. Early travel between Fort Erie and Port Maitland, whether by water or crude lakeshore trail, meant that a number of hotels and taverns would need to be built. Rathfon, a stone one-time hotel overlooking the lake, dates from 1797 and still stands as a private home. It lies to the east of Lowbanks. The Lowbanks community evolved around the Furry Tavern, which was built in 1821 by Lawrence and Barbara Furry and remained in that family until 1920. Today it retains much of its interior woodwork and sports a heritage plaque.

With the arrival of the Buffalo and Lake Huron Railway in the 1850s, a short distance to the north, tourists began to arrive at the shoreline while cottagers began to erect a string of summer homes. Because the shallow waters hindered boat access, a short railway branch line extended to the beach front from the main line. But unlike other sections of the shoreline farther east, beachfront development never completely overwhelmed Lowbanks.

In many places the road hugs the water's edge where the headstones of the village cemetery overlook the shore. The Bethesda church, now privately owned, dates from 1903. Other early structures, such as the general store and the United Church, built in 1866, as a Presbyterian church, can be seen along the stretch, as well, including at least one farm bearing a century farm sign.

Lowbanks is on Haldimand Road 3 about twelve kilometres east of Dunnville.

Selkirk

One of the area's oldest settlements, Selkirk began with the purchase by David Hoover of ten farm parcels along the Erie shore, west of the mouth of the Grand River, in 1800. The Hoovers soon built mills on the stream known as Stoney Creek. In 1827, David sold the land to William Steele who laid out the first village lots and named the place Williamsville in honour of himself. When the first post office opened in 1836, it adopted the name of the township, Walpole.

A hotel was added in 1833, and a store the following year. By 1855, the village had grown large enough to warrant its own post office, which took the name of the Earl of Selkirk, who in 1808 had purchased more than 30,000 hectares of land from the Six Nations, although he never paid the full agreed-to price. By 1875, the community could claim a variety of mills, stores, shops, and even a photographer and a brass band. That same year, R.J. Winyard opened a store in an attractive brick building at the northwest corner of the main intersection. It was taken over by the Bank of Hamilton in 1906 and continues to function as the CIBC.

A small fishery was operated by Walter Wheeler at nearby Horseshoe Bay. But the town's biggest industrial claim to fame was its centre as a natural gas producer. In 1904, a body of natural gas was discovered beneath the flat land surrounding the village. Although the existence of the gas field was known as early as 1867, it was only in 1892 that the government hailed the site as the area's largest gas-producing territory in Ontario up to that time.

Selkirk's Drilling Rig Museum recounts the days of the area's forgotten gas industry.

In 1905, the Dominion Natural Gas Company showed up, laying conductor lines and shipping gas to places like Hamilton, Galt, and Brantford. Before long, more than 150 gas wells operated around the Selkirk area. Whenever a gas well gushed forth, teamsters would move the drilling rig to the site. Four to six teams of workhorses strained to haul the rig, which was moved on skids and could weigh up sixteen tonnes.

A teamster's daily wage in the early days was a mere two dollars, but by the 1920s rose to more respectable six dollars. Over the years, several gas companies operated the Selkirk fields, despite the incredible depth of drilling required, as much as three hundred metres below the surface. The largest of the wells was uncovered in 1936 and contained a yield of 33,000 cubic metres. In 1959, the Place Gas and Oil Company could still count fifty wells operating in its 120-square-kilometre tract, most of it offshore.

Although most gas extraction ended in 1968, the community's motto continues to be: "By gas we live." This heritage is also celebrated each year by a "gas fest" and the informative Canada Drilling Rig Museum where the showpiece is a twenty-metre 1896-era wooden derrick. The restored drilling rig is a "fully working reconstruction of a natural gas drilling rig that worked in Haldimand and Norfolk in the 1930s," according the museum's handout. A group of local heritage enthusiasts discovered the remnants of the rig partly buried in mud near Milton and, after replacing the rotted wood, restored it to its original appearance.

While it is common for villages this size to have a local school, that in Selkirk is an architectural rarity. Built in 1917, the red brick "continuation" school, which taught students from grades one through twelve, has an unusually elaborate facade and a steeply pitched roof with a large central gable and a pair of dormers. In 1967, the school was converted into the area's community centre and has since been designated a heritage structure.

The road south from the main intersection leads to the "Blue Water Parkway," a scenic lakeshore drive which also follows the wooded banks of Stoney Creek. Selkirk is on Haldimand Road 3 about halfway between Dunnville and Port Dover.

Nanticoke

While the Blue Water Parkway is interrupted by Selkirk Provincial Park, a shoreline route, known as the South Coast Road, accessible at the south end of Brooklin Road, County Road 62, continues the shoreline drive. However, it soon brings into view to the west, one of Lake Erie's more unfortunate visions, the stacks of the Nanticoke Thermal Power Plant, said to be one of the single most polluting sources on the entire lake.

The industries began arriving in the late 1960s as part of a government initiative to decentralize urban growth from the burgeoning golden Horseshoe area. Ten years later, the initiative stalled, and the shore of Lake Erie was left with this unfortunate result. Today, the stacks and the structures of the Lake Erie Steel Company, Ontario Hydro, and the Imperial Oil Nanticoke refinery utterly dominate the landscape.

Overwhelmed now by the industrial area, the forgotten little village of Nanticoke itself lies on the banks of Nanticoke Creek. Here, the water-power site attracted early millwrights, and between 1830 and 1850 the village grew to add three hotels, four general stores, and three blacksmiths. In 1846, W.H. Smith's *Canadian Gazeteer* described Nanticoke as "a small village about 3/4 mile from the lake. It contains about 100 inhabitants and an Episcopal church, one gristmill, one sawmill, one store, one tannery, one tailor and one shoe-maker." By 1872, Abram Hoover had started a fishery at the mouth of the creek and in the 1950s the same family was still operating a pair of eighteen-metre fishing boats. They were joined by the Jackson brothers, who also operated fishing boats out of the little harbour.

Today, with industry looming on all sides, the fishing docks have become the Hoover Marina, while the fishing shanties have been renovated to house a popular local eatery, the Wharfside Restaurant. Back up in the village, more than a kilometre from the lake, two early churches still stand, and several early homes continue to occupy the small grid network of streets. One such heritage home, a farmhouse known as the Low Morrow house, a short distance west of the village, was acquired by Stelco and is preserved in the "green belt" that surrounds its factory. A fine example of an early farm home, it was built by Arthur Low in the 1870s.

Nanticoke sits about seven kilometres east of Port Dover, a little west of Haldimand Road 3.

Port Ryerse

Three gullies close together along the Erie shore all yield heritage villages, which, once bustling, are now little more than ghosts of their former prosperity.

The name of this hidden treasure trove of heritage buildings is richly deserved, for the founding Ryerse family was involved in almost every aspect of the little port's growth and a surprising amount of that heritage still lingers along the narrow hillside streets. In 1796, two Loyalist brothers, Joseph and Samuel Ryerson, received 1,200 hectares of land near the mouth of Young's Creek, six kilometres west of Port Dover. The condition was that Samuel

Nanticoke's one-time fishing sheds have evolved into a popular local restaurant, while the hydro stacks loom in the background.

Ryerse would undertake to build a saw and gristmill at the site. Both were badly needed to satisfy the early needs of the pioneer settlers, whom the government hoped to lure. Ryerse laid out a townsite with names like King Street, Rolph Street, Commercial Street, and William Street.

In 1813, the American invasion force, led by Colonel Campbell, which had just finishing scorching Port Dover, turned their torches to Port Ryerse, where they burned the mills and homes of the struggling settlers.

While Sam Ryerse immediately rebuilt the highly profitable sawmill (he kept half of everything he cut), he didn't bother to reconstruct the gristmill. In fact it was not until 1849 when another Ryerse brother, George, built a new gristmill on his land. In 1835, Edward P. Ryerse opened his brickyards, using his own products to build a house with walls that were four bricks thick in the event of another American attack.

By the 1850s, schooner-loads of gypsum were making their way down the Grand River Canal from the gypsum mines along the river's banks, and

Port Ryerse's Memorial Church dates from the times when the community was a busy industrial centre and port.

Ryerse added a plaster mill to the gristmill (the plaster was used to fertilize fields and was especially beneficial for clover). After the mill burned in 1860, Ryerse sold the site to Edward Harris and Joseph Potts, whose mill survived until the 1890s, when it also burned.

As early as 1835, steamers began calling at Port Ryerse's crude wharf for wood (this was the era before steamers began using coal). As a result, Edward P. Ryerse began to improve the harbour. To accommodate vessels of deeper drafts, he established the Simcoe and Port Ryerse Harbour Company and extended the wharf far into the lake. The growing inland town of Simcoe also used the port as its nearest shipping point. Although the boats could take on cargo by the warehouses on shore, the water was too shallow for them to take on a full load. They would need to go to the end of the wharf for heavier loads shuttled out to them by small tram cars. In 1871 alone, Port Ryerse shipped more than 2.5 million metres of timber and lumber products. Another of the key products shipped prior to 1844 was the pig iron being produced in the nearby iron furnaces in the village of Normandale.

Between 1860 and 1864, Port Ryerse became a minor shipbuilding centre with David Foster and William H. Ryerse building a number of schooners and scows with names like the *Brittania*, the *E.P. Ryerse*, and the *Georgiana*. It did not, however, develop into a major fishing centre with only the occasional American fishing boat setting their pound nets in the waters offshore.

During its heady days, Port Ryerse could boast a population of three hundred, with its mills, a store built in 1835, Stalker's blacksmith shop, and three hotels: the Port Ryerse Hotel, the Collins Hotel, and the Cutting Hotel. In 1867, Ryerse's harbour company expanded its mandate to include the building of a railway from Simcoe, but in 1872, the railway builders chose Port Dover, with its bigger harbour and land base over Port Ryerse, and the little port's dream of becoming a major shipper died.

Now overshadowed by Port Dover, a short distance to the east, Port Ryerse's days of prosperity began to fade. However, by the end of the century, the residents of Simcoe began to look to the little beach as a summer retreat, and, in 1910, the lakeshore was subdivided for cottages.

Today, with road improvements and the general trend toward countryside living, Port Ryerse has become a desirable residential community. Many new homes line its network of village streets. The long piers have long disappeared beneath the waves, although the structure remains in place closer to the shore; the mill site is no longer identifiable and two of the three hotels have gone. The historic store that stood until recently has been replaced with a newer home.

But history abounds along those quiet shady lanes. The Cutting Hotel still stands on King Street, known now as Idlewylde. The white frame gothic Memorial Church, built in 1870, still offers sermons, and the graves of the Ryerses stand quietly at the rear of the building, along with a plaque that commemorates them and the pioneers who built the community. Many heritage homes line Rolph Street with number 26 having been built as early as 1812. Number 16 dates from 1830 and number 27 from 1825, was built by a ship's captain. A home built by George G. Ryerse in 1866 still stands at number 22. And high on a hill in the centre of the village, the two-storey brick home, built by brickmaker E.P. Ryerse in 1836, still stands and has been declared a heritage structure. Commercial Street still leads to the shore where a number of early cottages still soak in the lake breezes and where locals can cast a fishing line off the remains of the piers.

Fishers Glen

A short distance west of Port Ryerse, another wooded gully cuts into the Lake Erie shore cliff. Like any other water-power site, the valley attracted an early mill. First named Newport, it later became Finch's Mills. As in Port Ryerse and Port Dover, the invading force of Americans burned the mill. In 1825, Finch sold the property to Thomas Cross and Don Fisher and the community began to ship out lumber, giving it the name Cross and Fisher's Landing.

But the decision to put the railway in Port Dover put an end to the shipping. In 1882, recognizing the growing appeal of the Lake Erie shore to vacationers, a three-storey hotel was built, complete with water fountains, miniature lakes, and waterfalls. Tourists began to seek out what was now being called Fishers Glen, with its tennis courts, croquet pitches, and merry-go-round.

Today, the little gully is lined with summer cottages and permanent homes, where private lanes now trace the old roads to the shore. Where today's road circles the head of the gully, an older house and small parkette mark the site of the early mills.

Normandale

The remains of Normandale lie in a valley that once held Ontario's busiest iron maker. As William H. Smith noted in his 1846 *Canadian Gazetteer*, the village, settled some twenty-five years previous, contained a "blast furnace for smelting iron ore … supplied with bog ore from the surrounding area (where) three or four thousand tons of ore have been found within the space of a few acres." He went on to observe that the ore would yield to 35 percent of iron worth between two and three dollars per tonne. "The furnace," he added, "is kept in operation about ten months in the year and when in blast produces about four tons of iron per day." The furnaces produced not only iron ore, but a cupola furnace turned out "castings of all descriptions."

The operation began around 1810 when English ironmaster John Mason began building a smelter on the small creek. He soon sold the operation to Hiram Capron (who would later found Paris, Ontario), George Tillson (after whom Tillsonburg is named), and Joseph Van Norman. Following the

Normandale's Union Hotel dates from the days when the place was Ontario's iron-producing capitol.

departure of the former two, Van Norman carried on the operation and the town adopted his name.

On the wall of the gully formed by the creek, the furnace consisted of a thirty-metre-high brick chimney, a water wheel, and a pair of bellows where the molten iron was poured into moulds.

At its peak, the town's population stood at about three hundred. However, by the mid-1840s, the supply of both bog ore and timber was quickly vanishing and Van Norman sold the furnace to John Shaw and went off to try his luck with the iron deposits at Marmora, Ontario. In the 1860s, Shaw built a flour and gristmill in place of the furnace, and added a wharf at the lake where a small fleet of fishing boats operated.

Even though no trace remains of any of the furnaces, wharves, or mills, Normandale's streets house a treasure trove of heritage buildings. The most prominent of those cluster at the main intersection of Main Street and Normandale Road. Here, standing side by side, are the former Union Hotel, which dates from the 1830s, and a diminutive boomtown-style store that once held the post office and general store. East of the hotel there stands a brick former Methodist church, now a residence, and a renovated one-time fisherman's home. From the intersection, Mill Street leads down the gully, past the site of the vanished mill (and of a vanished historic plaque that once commemorated it), and on to the lakeshore, which is now a quiet beach area.

West of the intersection one finds some of the town's early homes, including, on the northwest corner, the two-storey home of Richard Ferris, built during the furnace days, and immediately west of the current general store is the celebrated regency cottage-style home built by Romaine van Norman, Joseph's son. Its cupola and wraparound porch with French doors have been frequently featured in architectural magazines. The small cabins of the former furnace or mill workers are readily identifiable, as is the two-storey building at the corner of Hill Street, once known as the Red Tavern.

Normandale is on Front Road a short distance east of Norfolk Road 10.

St. Williams

While the village core resembles more a farm crossroads than a Lake Erie port, it did go by the name of "Port Metcalfe" as early as 1846, when it contained a Methodist church, a store, tavern, wagon maker, and a blacksmith. Most of these, however, were grouped around the intersection that went by a separate name, Neale's Corners. It was first settled in the early 1800s when the Cope, Procunier, and Price families took up lots around the intersection. Cope's Landing on the lake allowed for the shipping of lumber and grain. Its present name of St. Williams is said to honour a local landowner and religious leader named William Gellassy. When the Norfolk and Southern Railway established its link from Simcoe to Port Rowan, St. Williams earned a small station from which farm products were shipped to Simcoe.

In the 1870s, St. Williams was described as a pleasant village, which by then contained three stores, a hotel, three churches, and several tradesmen. McCall, McBurney and Co. operated a planning mill, shingle mill, and carriage shop. The main street was said to contain several very beautiful private residences —a few of which still survive. Today, although newer businesses have opened on the main street, it does retain a prosperous ambience of its earlier days. Two of the village's more historic buildings

The railway station at St. Williams was small but frequently busy.

Photo courtesy of Al Patterson.

include the 1866 St. Williams Anglican church, and the gothic brick 1865 farmhouse of Duncan McCall and Hannah Shearer, from which McCall operated a boatbuilding business.

While the heart of the village remains at the crossroads, all signs of the railway have vanished. At the shore, about two kilometres south, little remains of its shipping days. The wharf is now the centre of an ice fishing operation and is wedged between two large marinas. There is no general access to the shore.

Troyer

In 1793, John Troyer arrived from Pennsylvania and settled on a bluff atop the Lake Erie shore, a short distance east of Port Rowan. Here he carved out a farmstead, and created a small port with a dock, gristmill, blacksmith shop, and his own boat. However, because the creek on which he erected his mill flowed with so little water, the mill lasted only a few years.

But Troyer remains best remembered as being the area's first doctor. Self-taught, he was never medically trained. He planted and carefully harvested an herb garden, using the products to concoct potions for local settlers. Eventually, his psychic abilities earned him a reputation as a "witch" doctor. A superstitious man, he would hang horseshoes over his door, and was said to set bear traps to catch "witches." He was also in high demand as a water diviner, and reputedly found a chest of gold using only a Bible and candles.

The Troyer legend that has lingered the longest was his advice to a farmer whose family had been plagued by vandalism, crop failures, and fires, all attributed to a nearby woman who continuously threatened them. Troyer advised the beleaguered farmer to find and shoot a noisy goose with a silver bullet. After wounding the goose in the wing, the bothersome woman emerged with a broken arm, and the threats and ill fortunes ended.

Although Troyer lived to the age of eighty-nine, his commercial endeavours failed. Today an historic plaque — erected by the Port Rowan-South Walsingham Heritage Association — and the family graves still sit on the land where the "witch doctor" first settled.

Port Royal

This one-time port with the intriguing name, situated about six kilometres west of Port Rowan, began as an early shipping point on Big Creek, some distance upstream from Long Point Bay. In the 1840s, it possessed a steam sawmill, store, a pair of taverns, and a blacksmith. In the 1870s, it was being described as "a very old village [which] in the days when lumbering was active ... was an important place. But of late years business has declined to some extent."[1]

The Norfolk and Southern Railway chose Port Rowan as its Lake Erie terminus as Port Royal lacked suitable terrain and was hampered by a harbour that was too small. But it soon began to appeal to sportsmen. "The marshes are well supplied with game," the description goes on, "and sportsmen regard Port Royal as a desirable centre for their operations." Near Port Royal, Big Creek feeds into the extensive Long Point marshes, an area which has long attracted hunters.

An abandoned farm house near Port Royal shows why this area can be called a "ghost coast."

Today, the string of old houses is barely extensive enough to earn its highway sign. A sideroad leads north to the little cemetery, but at the creek itself, no evidence remains to tell of its busier period long ago.

Clear Creek

As Lakeshore Road continues west from Port Royal, the vestiges of the settlement of Clear Creek come into view. This hamlet developed on the shore road with a dock a short distance south on the lake. During its shipping period it could count two lumber merchants, a general store, blacksmith, and flour and gristmill. Its population was at one time estimated at one hundred.

Today, a side road still leads toward the former landing, but now, rather than pioneer cabins, modern homes line the route, while at the lake, access is blocked. A few businesses cluster around the intersection, among them the general store that continues to operate.

Houghton

Six kilometres west of Clear Creek, this now-vanished village developed along the road as an administrative centre for Houghton Township. Among its businesses were Jackson's general store and hotel, all in the same structure, three sawmills, along with blacksmiths and carpenters and the usual range of shops for a pioneer village. A cheese factory operated nearby, while the Baptist congregation added a solid brick church. Today, modern homes have replaced the vacant lots and simple cabins of Houghton's heyday. What was the hotel and store has been modernized and is now a residence, while the church has survived as a place of worship.

While Houghton was once the centre of the township, today it has become the centre of two unusual features. Rather than tall pines, the landscape around the ghost town stretches beneath nearly sixty whirring, giant wind turbines, each capable of generating 1,500 kilowatts of electricity. The Erie Shore Wind Farm will eventually incorporate more than 5,000 hectares of farmland and will feed 278,000 megawatt hours of energy into Ontario's electric grid.

Close by lies a feature considerably more ancient than the wind turbines, an enormous sand delta on the Lake Erie shore. During the retreat of the

Most of Houghton's "ghostly" structures have now been renovated or replaced by more modern homes.

last ice age, a massive river poured sand-laden water into a much higher predecessor of Lake Erie. As the lake level became lower, the edge of the massive delta began to erode and today has left a sand cliff that towers 120 metres above the lake. The authors of the early Norfolk County atlas enthused that there is "nothing more astonishing than the immense mound of pure sand standing upon the edge of the precipitous cliffs which border the lake."

During the nineteenth century, an eighteen-metre observatory was placed on its summit, which, along with similar structures at Long Point and in Pennsylvania, allowed for triangulation measurements. In the 1890s, an American glass manufacturer offered to buy the sand for his glass-making, but the natural treasure was rescued by George Alton, the owner of the property, who recognized its value as a natural attraction, and opened the site to visitors. Today the hills remain protected in a private campground.

Port Bruce

Compared to other Lake Erie ports, like Port Ryerse and Port Maitland, Port Bruce was a decided latecomer, although the site was known to Sir William Johnson, superintendent of Indian Affairs in Upper Canada. It was on the site of Port Bruce in 1761, during the Seven Years' War, that he ordered a Royal salute to commemorate the victories by the British at Belle Island in the Detroit River.

More than seventy years later, in 1835, local landowner, Henry Dalley, who owned harbourside property, pushed the government to recognize Port Bruce as a harbour, and invest in its improvements. However, it wasn't until the 1840s that the mouth of Catfish Creek began to see any shipping. Then, in 1851, Lindley Moore and Amasa Lewis bought a tract of land along the river and laid out the port of Port Bruce. Their town plan depicts a market square upstream, around which a network of streets and town plots was designed. Near the mouth of the creek another network of streets and building lots appeared. Between the two lay a high hill considered at the time to repel easy development.

Lewis and Moore concentrated on shipping grain or peas to Quebec. Near the wharf, Lewis, along with Stephen Davis and Captain Thomas Thompson, operated grain elevators. Several sawmills cut timber along the banks of the creek. To more easily move the logs to the mills, they were often dragged to

Elgin County Archives, 1893, ECVF, Box 1, File 6.

An early view of Port Bruce from the east hill shows how it was once a busy harbour.

the top of the hill and rolled down the slope to the mills below. Unfortunately, the sawdust from the mills silted up the river mouth, decimating the budding fishery. Despite the siltation problems, Sylvanus Young and his sons operated the port's leading fishery for several years.

Because the mouth of the creek was shallow in any event, Lewis extended a pier 130 metres into the lake, while the government chipped in $6,000 to improve the harbour. In 1876, a frame lighthouse was built at the end of the pier; a frame shanty with a tripod for the light mounted on top.

To help move farm produce to the port, a private consortium built a gravel road from Aylmer to the lake, installing the hated toll booths along the way. But by then things were on a downward slide in the little port. The railways had passed it by and the timber was running out. The road was taken over by the township, and, in 1874, the tolls were eliminated. But the beach area was soon discovered by nearby townsfolk and Port Bruce started to become a recreation mecca.

As it grew as a port, the village acquired two hotels, Hewitt and Parker's hotel near the bridge, and the Commercial Hotel by the harbour. While the bridge hotel burned in the 1870s, the Commercial Hotel kept pace with tourism and, in 1882, the name was changed to the Lakeview and then again, in 1913, to the King George. In 1932, the building was moved back from the

Port Bruce's Rocabore Inn is one of the village's oldest structures dating from the days when it was a busy harbour.

water's edge and the wraparound porch replaced. The name, too, was changed once more and it became the Rocabore Inn, named after the mythical Irish goat creatures. The building still stands today.

Atop the prominent hill in the centre of the town stands the village's most historic home. With its elegant captain's walk (or "widow's walk" as the belvedere is depressingly called), the grand home was built for his wife in 1860 by the village's founder, Amasa Lewis. Inside it retains its high ceilings, fireplaces, and circular staircase. Originally known as "Whitehall," today it is the Port Bruce Manor, a thirty-six-bed adult assisted-living facility.

In 1929, one of the village's more unusual summer homes was added. The grand-niece of inventor Thomas A. Edison built a miniature castle inspired by the castle image on the tins of Turret cigarettes. Although it first had a moat, it is now surrounded by a lawn and plants. Edison himself, although born in Milan, Ohio, was a frequent visitor to his grandfather's home in nearby Vienna. The little "castle" sits on Hale Street behind the hotel.

The layout of Port Bruce still resembles that in the original town plan of Amasa and Lewis. A collection of houses, old and new, line the bridge area, while newer homes on larger lots now crown the hilltops. Smaller and older homes, along with seasonal cabins, line Main and Hale Streets by the wharf. A provincial park has taken over the shoreline, and with it has come a small number of take-out restaurants and gift shops. The lighthouse was replaced in 1953 with a six-metre circular tower surmounted by a green flashing light. Otherwise, all evidence of industrial activity has gone. The pier-side buildings have all been removed and in their place stretches Wonnacutt Park, where fishermen cast their lines from the dock where the schooners once called. Meanwhile, a new marina and private docks now line Catfish Creek up to the bridge.

Port Bruce, however, had a predecessor, a village called either Davenport or Devonport. In 1817, Colonel John Hale and his son Edward acquired more than a half-dozen land parcels west of present-day Port Bruce. Here, they laid out a street pattern and added a store, hotel, blacksmith shop, and tailor. The success of Devonport, however, depended upon the government cutting a channel from the lake to Catfish Creek farther upstream. When the mouth of Catfish Creek proved to be more suitable for a harbour, the notion of a canal was dropped and Devonport's few buildings were moved to the new port.

Port Bruce is on Elgin Road 73, seventeen kilometres south of Aylmer, and twenty-two kilometres west of Port Burwell.

Jamestown

Prior to the growth of Port Bruce, Jamestown flourished as a mill town a short distance upstream. In 1835, a land speculator from St. Thomas, James Chrysler, recognized the value of the timber and had the site laid out in village lots where he built saw and gristmills along with a distillery. Lumber and grain were loaded onto scows and floated downstream to the mouth of the creek, where, before the piers were built at Port Bruce, they were barged out to ships waiting offshore.

As the mill village grew, Jamestown added a hotel, store, blacksmith, and wagon shop with about ten houses. But with the disappearance of the timber, and increasing taxes on whisky, Jamestown began to slide downhill. While the sawmill was later converted to a flax mill for the manufacture of paper and linen, the remaining mill buildings were removed and the hotel was converted into a private residence. Most evidence of the once-bustling village washed away in flood waters in 1937.

As the Jamestown Line descends into the pastoral little valley there remains nothing to demonstrate that this place was once busier than Port Bruce.

Port Talbot

Despite the fact that this port played such a key role in the development of Lake Erie in this area, nothing of it remains. The rural community which surrounds the site, however, still retains many of the early homesteads.

And it all goes back to one the area's best-remembered personalities, Colonel Thomas Talbot. Born in Malahide Castle north of Dublin, Ireland, Talbot enlisted in the Duke of Wellington's 24th Regiment and became the private secretary of Governor John Graves Simcoe, lieutenant governor of Upper Canada. After returning to England, Talbot convinced the government to allow him to implement a land settlement scheme along the shore of Lake Erie. The government allotted him 2,000 hectares and agreed to award him eighty hectares for every settler he attracted.

In 1803, Talbot arrived at the mouth of Talbot Creek and built a log cabin. Nearby he added a sawmill, a cooper shop, a blacksmith shop, and a poultry house, along with a barn. When settlers began to arrive in 1809, Talbot added a gristmill, as well. In 1813, along with virtually all other mills along the shore, the Americans invaders burned the Talbot mill, along with his first log home. Talbot himself barely escaped capture by fleeing to a neighbouring house disguised, it is said, in women's clothes. Anticipating a raid, Talbot, who was in charge of the local militia defence during the War of 1812, had built a pair of small forts one on the water, the other on a nearby ridge. But the tiny force was no match for the Americans and its members fled.

A new home soon appeared, which Talbot named the "Hermitage." There is local controversy as to whether or not Talbot himself built and lived in the mansion, or whether it was erected and occupied by a nephew, Colonel Richard Airey. Whatever the case, Talbot eventually moved to London where he lived until his death in 1853.

For several years there was not much more to Port Talbot than Talbot's buildings. By 1881, Talbot Macbeth, a neighbouring landowner, had built a sawmill and a dock with a grain warehouse from which he shipped grain and

Ontario Archives, RG 26-G-961.

A rare view of Thomas Talbot's Hermitage in its later years before demolition.

lumber. For a time, the bay sported a small fishery, as well. Later, gravel from the beach was extracted for use on that area's roads. A photograph taken in the 1940s shows a few buildings still standing by the water's edge. However, the shallow waters kept most vessels far offshore where smaller boats took the cargo to them, and activity at the failing port soon ceased.

The "Hermitage" passed through various hands, including a Detroit syndicate that envisioned a resort complex for the site. In 1997, the historic house, then derelict, was demolished. The property remains in private hands, although a roadside cairn just west of the gated entrance commemorates the significance of Thomas Talbot and his port.

The final vestiges of the legacy of the port are the homes and farms of Talbot's settlers that can be found in the surrounding area. Along Lake Road to the west of Port Talbot is the St. Peter's Anglican Church, built in 1837. In the cemetery across the road lie the remains of Talbot himself, as well as those of many of Port Talbot's earliest residents. A short distance east of the church, a two-storey white wooden farmhouse was built by Leslie Patterson, a retired colonel, in 1827, and is the oldest building in the settlement. Close by and on

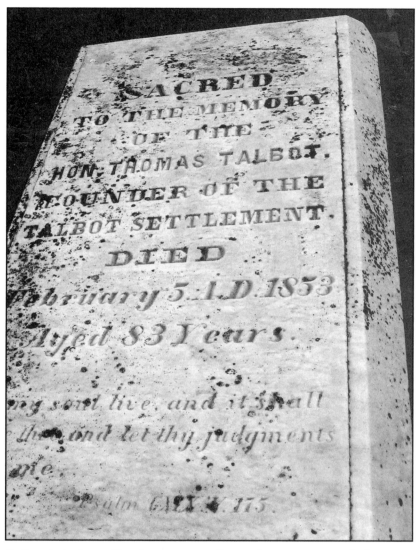

St. Peter's Anglican Church near Port Talbot and its cemetery mark the resting place of colonizer, Thomas Talbot.

the north side of the road, a long white frame two-storey house was that of Patterson's brother-in-law, Stephen Backus, and dates back to 1830.

West of the church is one the area's best preserved homes, and one of the first built with brick, the Backus-Page house. Built for Andrew and Mary Jane Backus in 1850 by Andrew Morris, who used 72,000 bricks, it is now a museum operated by the Tyrconnell Heritage Society. The Backus-Page House museum is open daily to the public between June 1 and Labour Day except Mondays.

One of the pioneers who arrived during the Talbot years was John Pearce, who fled across Lake Erie in a small boat, struggling to make shore. A little west of the Backus-Page home, in 1809, he built his own homestead. The property, along with his home, remains in the Pearce family to this day and the John Pearce Provincial Park is named in his honour.

But Talbot's legacy extended far beyond the boundaries of his settlement. Deputy surveyor for Upper Canada Mahlon Burwell laid out some of the area's earliest pioneer roads, including the Talbot Road, which led east from Port Talbot to Delhi in 1809, and west from the settlement of Talbotville near St. Thomas to Sandwich (now Windsor) in 1811.

Talbot's name is celebrated in the name of St. Thomas and the nearby community of Talbotville Royale. His mark even extends to London, Ontario, where, while serving on the commission to design the new London court-house, he convinced the commissioners to design it after his beloved Mala-hide Castle in Ireland.

Tyrconnell

While any semblance of a village at Port Talbot was vanishing, a new town was appearing a short distance west. Following the war of 1812, Buller and Haynes built a gristmill on the lower section of Number 9 Creek. This was to replace the mill burned at Port Talbot. A short distance upstream, Colby added a saw-mill. At first, the growing community was named Little Ireland.

In 1852 James Blackwood subdivided the land into two hundred lots all grouped around twenty village streets and the post office took the name Tyrconnell. With some protection offered by the mouth of Number 9 Creek, he constructed a wharf and warehouse to ship grain. In 1861, the Dunwich Pier Company added a 150-metre-long pier to allow the larger schooners to load grain without having to send smaller boats to the shore. The harbour soon developed a small fishery. Tyrconnell's prosperity peaked in the 1870s when a business directory described it as "favourably located for manufacturing purposes," and listed its population as four hundred. Among its businesses were the Tyrconnell House and the Globe Hotel, along with John Mitchell's flour and gristmills, and William Morden's tannery as well as stores, blacksmiths, and the usual variety of early shops. According to the business directory "large amounts" of grain were shipped by Meredith Conn.

With the arrival of the railways at Port Stanley, and the need to accommodate larger steamers, the fishery and the grain shipping at Tyrconnell ended. Businesses moved away, and the place became a ghost town. A few of the twenty village streets still are visible, including Erie Street, which leads to the lake. Here, a large concrete abutment is all that survives of the pier. Grassy meadows tell of the warehouse site. The village's one-time town hall still stands on George Street, while on Hill Street a house that sports a columned porch was once a lodge.

Tyrconnell can be found at the end of Elgin Road 6, eleven kilometres south of Dutton.

Little remains at the once busy port of Tyrconnell other than a few early homes and the remains of the pier.

Eagle

While many of the shoreline roads were collapsing into the crashing waters of Lake Erie, the Talbot Line ran safely parallel to the shore about one-and-a-half kilometres inland. Like many of the shoreline villages in this area, Eagle had a twofold landscape. While shipping facilities appeared at the shore, the main village began to grow along the road itself.

Eagle began to develop around a mill on Brock's Creek, the village's first name, around 1855. William Mowbray built a sawmill by the shore, where staves were lowered down a series of grooves in the bluff. In 1863, a dock was added, and the following year Eagle was laid out as a village, taking its new name, according to local lore, from a family of nesting eagles. As it grew, the village acquired five hotels, including the Elgin Hotel and the Dominion House, as well as the renowned Eagle Hotel, built by Fred Lindenman in 1874.

During the Fenian raids of the 1860s, a hotel, owned by one Livingston, received some unwelcome visitors. A small band of American soldiers, sent to arrest any Fenians they could catch, arrived asking for room and board. Livingston refused to give them rooms or to accept their American currency. Instead, the troops were obliged to buy their drinks with any valuables they were carrying and, after several drinks, were grateful to sleep in the barn. After they had continued on their way, Livingston found that he had come upon a windfall of four hundred dollars' worth of jewellery.

When the railways passed farther inland through Dutton and West Lorne, the villages along the shore became backwaters. The Eagle Hotel and the general store managed to survive that downturn, but are gone now. Eagle, however, remains an identifiable community, although newer buildings now crowd the intersection. Lakeview Gardens Greenhouse now attracts visitors much as the old hotels must have once done. A small conservation area, Feasby Park, at the end of Graham Road near the site of the early harbour, offers views along the Lake Erie shore.

Eagle is on the Talbot Line, Elgin Road 3, about a dozen kilometres west of Tyrconnell.

Port Glasgow

As the name might suggest, the earliest arrivals hailed from Scotland. In 1813, the Forbes, Gillies, and Haggart families, arriving by way of New York, were given their twenty-hectare allotment by Thomas Talbot, although Talbot frowned upon settlers who arrived via the United States. He assumed that such settlers were simply interested in the free land. And many were. A prominent nearby hill was given the name Nellie's Hill after another new arrival, Nellie Campbell. Now gone, this prominent landmark was later excavated for its sand deposit. The next name given the fledgling settlement was Port Furnival.

A small, protected cove beneath the hilltop hamlet offered a harbour for the first shipments, although the initial dock was simply a wharf that extended into the lake below the hill. Later on, the creek was dredged and a pier was built to allow large vessels to call. As the village grew, a small street network was laid out where, in the late 1820s, the Royal George Hotel and MacFarlane's store began their businesses. Close by were a shoemaker, cabinetmakers, and a blacksmith. MacFarlane was also the leading shipper and in 1859 was

Port Glasgow's modern marina keeps the port alive.

able to ship 6,000 bushels of wheat, 50 bushels of flax, and 120 barrels of pork, along with large quantities of deer and racoon skins.

Meanwhile, another community was evolving two kilometres north of the port on the Talbot Road. First surveyed by Sir Richard Airey in 1850, it was named Airey. Later renamed New Glasgow, it became the centre of the township's justice system, with the township clerk, a clerk of the divisional court, a bailiff, and two justices of the peace. In addition it could count a store, John Livingston's Commercial Hotel, and a saw and gristmill.

The road to the harbour today leads to a park and modern marina. On the hilltop, an historic plaque commemorates the "Aldorough pioneers and soldiers" next to which a community park overlooks the waters of the lake. The street pattern is now missing the store and hotel, but does still include a few older dwellings along with more modern residences. Back up on the highway, new businesses and homes have replaced nearly all the historic stores and houses which once were New Glasgow.

Clearville

Although it has now nearly faded from the landscape, Clearville was one of the earliest and most important of the settlements on this section of the lakeshore. Settlers began to arrive here as early as 1816 when John Colebrook Bury took up land. By 1817, the place had seen its first hotel, a crude log cabin that doubled as a town hall. Around 1830, a store opened close to the hotel and Clearville received its first post office. At that time the local name, Clear Creek, was changed to Clearville as there was another Clear Creek not far away. The community was also called Hanover, but that name, too, had been taken.

The Baldwin Hotel was replaced with a larger structure nicknamed "Dandy Hall" and "Baldwin's Castle." It served a variety of roles, including that of a town hall, election booth, auction hall, and centre of local business meetings. Municipal functions later moved on to the village of Duart and then eventually to the larger community of Highgate.

The harbour continued to be busy with a small shipbuilding operation where as many as forty labourers might work on a single ship. Passenger ships called at Clearville as well, taking revellers to places like Erie Beach or even across the lake to Cleveland. At the dock, warehouses stored grain and staves.

These storage buildings were later purchased by the Koehlers and converted to a fishpacking plant. The Koehlers sold the plant in 1954 to the Dawdy brothers. The catch consisted primarily of herring but could also include pickerel and perch, as well.

Aside from the harbour operations, most of Clearville's businesses were located two kilometres north on the Talbot Road. Here were two hotels, the Canada House and the Clearville Inn, and the Hanover Mills, a water-powered gristmill built in 1832 by Colonel George Henry and later operated by Bogart and Taylor. These buildings are now gone.

In 1964, the township purchased the harbour, cleared away the harbour buildings, and today the site is a municipal campground and trailer park. Little evidence has survived from Clearville's days as a Lake Erie port.

Clearville is nine kilometres west of New Glasgow on Elgin Road 3.

Antrim

Located at the mouth of Big Creek, a short distance south of Morpeth, Antrim was a short-lived but once active little port. The Big Creek formed what was in the day a well-regarded harbour. Among the first to recognize its potential were the Ruddle family, who in 1827 acquired title to the land on either side of the creek and opened a trading post, as there was no store in the area.

At the wharf, the Ruddles added a gristmill, a large warehouse, and a brick hotel, and surveyed lots on both sides of the creek. They named the site Antrim after their home parish in Ireland. The mysterious ruins of a pair of forts, whose origins are unknown, remained nearby, but eventually disappeared before the port came into its own. The harbour quickly became a busy shipping point with wagons lined up to deliver grain to the warehouse. A high-level bridge, which would allow ships' masts to pass beneath it, was built between the lake and the harbour. Four times a year farmers poured into the village for a popular cattle sale. During Antrim's heyday, a number of small schooners were built and launched in the harbour.

But the glory days would not last. Fewer than ten village lots were sold, and the township replaced the more costly high-level bridge with a low-level structure that was less expensive to maintain. As a result, the dock moved farther east where the road south from Morpeth met the lake. Known as Hill's Dock, it was named after the port's warfingers and leading merchants,

Erasmus and Austin Hill. For several years Morpeth's needs were shipped in through Hill's Dock and much of their farm produce shipped out. But eventually the quantities dwindled and the financially strapped dock was shut down.

Today the road still ends near the lake, but no evidence of the dock remains. The handsome two-storey Hill house still stands, however, as a testimony to the once-busy pair of little ports.

Still another dock operated at the end of the next road to the east and was known as Wilson's Dock and consisted of a store, hotel, dock, and warehouse. However, it lacked the protection of a creek and lasted for only a brief time.

Meanwhile, back up on the Talbot Road, Morpeth was prospering as a mill town and stagecoach stop with four hotels and mills. At one time it seemed as though a proposed railway would pass through Morpeth, but the scheme collapsed and the village never realized the dreams which the railways would have brought. Today it remains a substantial residential village, but the business district is only a ghost of what it was.

Shrewsbury

To those unfamiliar with its history, the street pattern in Shrewsbury would seem most unusual. Here in a flat and low-lying shoreline, on the north side of Rondeau Bay, lies a strict grid network of streets, clearly laid out with a grander purpose in mind than the scattering of today's modest homes would indicate.

Indeed it was intended to be. As lieutenant governor of Upper Canada, John Graves Simcoe had envisioned this well-protected harbour, known originally as Rondeau Harbour, as the site of the seat for a county named Suffolk, as well as providing an important shipping point. A road called the Communication Road would link it with Chatham, an important military town located on the Thames River. At a time when Simcoe was contemplating Chatham as Ontario's capital, along with London, the Communication Road and the harbour on Rondeau Bay would allow Chatham a safe alternative route for receiving military supplies should they be needed. The other route was the Thames River, navigable from Lake St. Clair to Chatham.

Although Upper Canada's deputy surveyor general, Abraham Iredell, surveyed the road and terminus in 1797, Chatham never became the capital first envisioned, and when the War of 1812 erupted, the terminus and road were not needed. Iredell's plan showed not only the grid of residential streets, but a reserve for a court house and market square. Streets were twenty-two metres wide, and the lots thirty-one metres wide and sixty-two metres deep,

However, that all changed during the 1840s when fugitive slaves began pouring along the Underground Railroad, and communities along the north shore of Lake Erie were a logical landing place, especially those with little local population to object. To provide enough lots for the newcomers, the first plan was resurveyed into smaller lots, and registered at Chatham in 1847. In 1848 it was named Shrewsbury after a town in Shropshire, England. At this time the streets acquired new names, those that they bear to this day: Wellington, Adelaide, Victoria, and Albert, names which in 1797 would have had no regal relevance.

Many refugees did take up the small parcels and found work building the harbour at Erieau, or establishing market gardens in the mucky black soil. But, beyond the community of former slaves, the settlement failed to grow in size or economy. No docks of any size were ever built, no railway arrived. Today, homes occupy many of the lots, few of them of any historic vintage, and Shrewsbury remains the image of a failed paper town.

However, a small dock was built a short distance to the east where a road angled toward the water. Here a grew a small village named Raglan, which contained Sewell's general store and the Hartford Hotel, as well as a sawmill and grain elevator. Today it is a small residential community.

Buckhorn

Today even the name no longer exists except on a store, but in 1880, Buckhorn thrived as a village of 250 with three stores, a hotel, a flour and shingle mill, and a barrel factory. The community began as a hotel stop on the Talbot Road when, in 1853, Nelson Chapman opened the Farmers House Tavern. When Chapman added a deer's head to his decorations, he renamed it the Buckhorn Tavern and the name spread to the village as well.

A road led a short distance south to the lake where the Buckhorn Dock and White Pigeon Hotel were built. In 1884, the name was changed to Cedar Springs in celebration of the cedar trees in the area and a spring of fresh water that the area residents used.

The railway age arrived in Cedar Springs with the building of the Lake Erie and Detroit River Railway (LE&DR) and the Wallaceburg, Chatham and

Lake Erie electric railway. The LE&DR built a station five kilometres north of Cedar Springs where a separate town site was laid out. However, by the time passenger service ended, and the station was closed, the townsite remained vacant. While the electric line had little impact on the village, it did bolster the market garden industry, shipping sugar beets from the drained marshes.

Located on Kent Road 3, five kilometres west of Blenheim, Cedar Springs remains a bustling village in this prosperous area of the Lake Erie shore.

Union and Albertville

The Lake Erie shoreline between Leamington and Kingsville can hardly qualify as a "ghost coast" as new homes and agricultural greenhouses crowd the roads, and cottages and homes form a solid line along the shore. Still, it was here, about three kilometres east of Kingsville, that the shore's busiest port once shipped out farm products and lumber. At the mouth of a small creek, a modest amount of water power allowed for the building of early mills. A post office opened in 1831, and by 1850 Albertville could claim a general store, school, log church, hotel, and grist and sawmills. Then, in the 1850s, when a larger dock was built at Union, two kilometres east of Albertville, shipping switched to that site.

Eventually, when the Lake Erie and Detroit River Railway was built into Kingsville with its larger harbour, and a station was established at Ruthven, a village a little more than a kilometre away, both Union and Albertville faded. Only the street patterns have survived the arrival of newer cottages and larger year-round homes.

Colchester

The area around Colchester began to develop as early as 1813 when John Snider, a blacksmith from Pennsylvania, built the area's first home. The first village business was the tavern of Edward Sinasac, erected in the 1840s on Dunn Road, which led from the Talbot Road to the lake. An extensive townsite was laid out, much of it eventually settled by fugitive slaves from the United States. It was described as a "wretched settlement."[3]

About a third of the population of Colchester consisted of the African-American refugees. Discrimination was harsh here, as police patrols routinely

The harbour at Colchester is now home only to pleasure craft.

kept the black population from using the public beaches. Soon, most had moved away to join larger populations of blacks in Windsor and Chatham, and to take up jobs on the railways.

That large-scale depopulation is reflected today in the town's appearance, with most of the central section of the village vacant. Only a convenience store and small café comprise the business "district," and the road to the harbour remains eerily empty. The harbour, however, now enlarged, is a different matter, with a flotilla of pleasure craft crowded into the slips. The naval battle of Put-in-Bay in 1813, a losing engagement for the British fleet, was fought just offshore. Today, another reminder that the United States is only a short distance away are the stacks of Ohio's infamous coal-fired electric plants that loom above the lake's distant blue horizon.

10

THE POINTS

Point Abino ~ Turkey Point ~ Long Point ~ Point aux Pins
Point Pelee ~ Pelee Island

While much of the Lake Erie shoreline displays a monotonous line of cliffs, these are interrupted by not just the river mouths which gave rise to bustling ports, but also by prominent points of land that jut into the lake, and which have played a significant role in the heritage of the Lake Erie shore. They have variously become important agriculture areas, ecological areas, recreational areas, or more gruesomely, graveyards for far too many ships.

Point Abino

Point Abino, a headland of sand and rock, stabs into the lake immediately west of Crystal Beach. Today it has become a site of considerable controversy. Both the point and the road that follows it are controlled by a group of wealthy American landowners known as the Point Abino Association. It would be just another foreign-owned gated community — except for one thing — at the very tip of the point stands one of the Great Lakes' most magnificent lighthouse stations. Although the Point Abino Lighthouse is now a national historic site, the Americans control who can visit and when, effectively restricting Canadians' right to see one their own national treasures.

Before the American "invasion," the sole occupant of the site had been Father Claude Aveneau, a Jesuit missionary to the local Native peoples, likely members of the Seneca tribe. Here, atop one the large dunes that form the backbone of the point, he built a log cabin. Following the arrival of the first

Point Abino's heritage lighthouse displays a rare classic style of architecture.

permanent settlers, a family known only as Dennis, the point evolved into a small industrial centre. During the last half of the nineteenth century, a saw-mill, a lime kiln, and a quarry with a short horse-drawn rail line to haul out the material, all operated on the point. A pair of boarding houses provided accom-modations for the workers.

By then the name had become a corruption of Father Aveneau's name and was known more simply as Point "Abino." Then, in 1892, Isaac Holloway, a Buffalo developer, acquired the point and subdivided the parcel into fifty lots, leaving twenty-eight as common land and sold the entire property to a group of twenty-one wealthy Buffalo businessmen who formed the Point

Abino Association. For several years, access to the point remained by means of a small launch, the *Marion L*, which plied the waters between Buffalo, Point Abino, and Crystal Beach. With the improvement to the road system and increasing car ownership, the yacht was retired and spent its last days as a tug in the harbour at Buffalo.

Today, this gated community displays a range of grand summer homes ranging from older, more traditional styles to modern architect-designed mansions. One of the more historic of the point's buildings is a home known formerly as the "Wisconsin House." Built in 1901 as the Wisconsin State Building for the Buffalo Pan-American Exposition, it was moved to the point when the Expo ended. It is distinguished by its Moorish-style windows, the front portion of which has now been covered by a subsequent addition.

The grand palaces of the Americans line the east shoreline, while the central portion of the peninsula is a ridge of sand dunes, and the west side of the ridge is a designated natural area. At the tip of the private point stands the magnificent Point Abino lighthouse. Built in 1917, the lighthouse replaced a lightship that had sunk in November 1913 during one of the lake's most vicious storms, its crew of six perishing with it. When it came time to build the new lighthouse, the federal government signed an agreement with the Point Abino Association that the lighthouse would remain accessible by water only. As a result, the building was constructed on a flat, rocky shelf beyond the ownership of the cottagers. Gravel for the concrete base had to be hauled, not along the private road, but along the more difficult west shore, while the first keepers were required to travel to the tower by water. The ruined pier remains visible near the tower.

Because of its location almost in the water, the base was higher than most lighthouses would require, while the tower stretched thirty metres above that. Despite its sturdy build, a vicious winter storm in 1985 sent waves crashing through the windows, filling the engine and watch room with more than a metre-and-a-half of cold water. When the storm finally abated, it had left behind a coating of ice a metre-and-a-half thick.

Known more properly as a "light station," the light tower did not contain a keeper's residence. That grand home, built in style consistent with the homes of the Americans, sits on the shore bluff well away from the waves. The tower itself, surrounded by a flat wave-washed limestone shelf, is unique among Great Lakes light towers for its classical lines and its poured-concrete construction. Automated in 1988, it was decommissioned in 1995, and declared a national heritage site. Despite federal policy that heritage properties should be accessible, the Americans kept this heritage treasure out of bounds. Finally, following years of debate, and sometimes acrimonious discussion with the cottagers' association, the Town of Fort Erie bought the historic structure in 2003 and obtained limited public access to it. Today, inside the main entrance, visitors can view historic photos and articles that recount the story of the lighthouse and its keepers. Here, too, remains the compressed air fog horn that warned ships away from the point's dangerous shoals.

While the road to the lighthouse remains in the hands of the Americans, and gated to keep out Canadians in cars, visitors on foot or bicycle are permitted during certain hours through the summer. (Some continue to dispute the private ownership of the road, suggesting that because of maintenance work having supposedly been done by the municipality, it should be opened as a public road.)

Meanwhile, hard at work to restore the crumbling old lighthouse, is a dedicated group of volunteers, known as the PALS (Point Abino Lighthouse Preservation Society), which, during the summer, runs scheduled shuttles full of history lovers out to see one of this country's most magnificent maritime structures. While visitors are reminded that photographing the homes is not permitted, at least no passports are required.

Turkey Point

Although Turkey Point forms part of the Long Point Biosphere Reserve, geographically it remains distinct, a sand spit stretching in a southwesterly direction, and an extensive marsh lies behind it. Along the spit, a dense agglomeration of homes and summer cottages mingles with an array of seasonal restaurants and shops. During the lake's warm summer days, the point teems with bathers enjoying the sandy beaches of Turkey Point Provincial Park, or pitching a tent, or golfing above the bluff.

The promontory drew the attention of John Graves Simcoe, who saw it as a strategic location for a fort and a new district capital. Because of the valuable timber above the point, Simcoe designated it as "naval reserve," and, to protect it, drew up plans for Fort Norfolk. The capital would be in a townsite named Charlotteville. The naval depot was briefly home to Commander Barclay's small Lake Erie fleet, consisting of the *General Hunter*, the *Queen Charlotte*, and the *Lady Prevost*.

The beach at Turkey Point is part of the provincial park.

But it was only after the tide began to turn against the British forces in southwestern Ontario with General Henry Proctor's demoralizing defeat at Amherstburg that construction on the fort belatedly began. Although the military failed to complete anything other than the fort's palisade, Charlotteville, for a brief period, contained a jail, a courthouse, and a small collection of ancillary dwellings. In 1813, however, all district functions were relocated to Vittoria, five kilometres north of Normandale, and the site fell silent. Today it lies beneath a golf course with only a cairn to commemorate its existence.

Most of Turkey Point, however, consists of an extensive marshland stretching from the bluff to the end of the sand spit. The marshes offer a haven for a wide variety of animal species, some of them endangered, although a small corner was drained for vegetable production, a role it still plays today. Atop the bluff, the Joseph W. Csubak Memorial Viewing Area[1] offers a view across the wide marshlands to the tree-lined sand spit.

Long Point

Visitors to Port Rowan may stand on the hilltop at the foot of the main street and read on a plaque about how a long line of trees across the bay stretching to the horizon became the first of Ontario's three UNESCO World Biosphere Reserves. That was in 1986, but the story of Long Point goes back much further.

As its name implies, Long Point is a forty-kilometre-long sand spit that stretches from the Lake Erie bluffs just west of Port Rowan southeasterly into the middle of the lake. Unusual in its length, it was formed by the easterly currents of the lake, gathering up sand and silt from the shoreline bluffs, and then meeting with the silt-laden waters of Big Creek at a point where the curvature of the shoreline causes the currents to slow. As they do, the debris falls to the bottom. Over the many centuries since the lake reached its current level, that deposit has built up into one of Ontario's most unusual natural features, and one of Lake Erie's most dangerous.

For most of its length, Long Point is an ecological mixture of marshes, sand dunes, and forests. However, close to the shoreline, the narrow neck, mostly marsh, offered a convenient portage for the early First Nations. Between its tip and the mainland, Long Point encloses a wide, shallow bay, which is also protected by Turkey Point. In these warm, shallow waters, many fish species breed. The site, as a result, was a popular gathering spot for the early tribes to stock up on their fish supply.

Long Point also lent its name to a large area along the shoreline, one that became known as the "Long Point Settlement." As the "Long Point" settlers cleared their land and planned their towns like Port Royal, Port Rowan, Normandale, and Port Ryerse, much of Long Point itself remained largely uninhabited. But it did not remain entirely free of human activity. Once the mainland had been stripped of its forests, and the marshes hunted out, illegal loggers and game poachers turned their attention to Long Point's forests and marshes. Because the government of the day placed low value on the sandy point, they withheld the resources necessary to control the unlawful activities. Then, in 1853, to establish some form of control, they sent surveyor James Black to survey the point and put it up for public auction.

At first there was little interest. Then, in 1866, a group of businessmen and hunters, calling themselves the Long Point Company, acquired the outermost 6,000 hectares. One of the conditions of the sale was that the company would be responsible for regulating and policing the point. They took their role seriously, and in less than a decade, fish and wildlife populations that had been nearly eradicated — especially deer and muskrat — were rebounding.

But resource exploitation was not the only problem on Long Point. The spit was also quickly earning a reputation as creating some of the most dangerous waters on the Great Lakes. Here, the point, in combination with fierce currents, sudden storms, and frequent fog, sent more ships to a watery grave in a much smaller area, than the infamous Bermuda Triangle, a phenomenon that earned these waters the nickname, the "Lake Erie Quadrangle." Here, in an area defined by Port Burwell and Port Dover on the Canadian side and Barcelona, New York, and Conneaut (Ohio) on the American side, more than 440 vessels were sunk. That compares to 112 in the Triangle, which is six times the area.

Among the more notable of the many sinkings was that of a ship called the *James B. Colgate*. With its enclosed whaleback design it was considered "unsinkable." Yet during one of the lake's hurricane-like storms, it began to list. As the hatchways gave out, the captain and crew abandoned the vessel. Only the captain survived, and the *James P. Colgate* was never seen again. But not all wrecks ended so tragically. In 1854, a vessel called the *Conductor* was washed aground. Abigail Becker, who lived in a nearby cabin, heard the telltale signs of sails flapping in the fierce winds. As she rushed to the shore she saw the eight-man crew clinging desperately to the masts. One by one she got them ashore and, with the help of her children, warmed them up with tea and blankets. As a reward she was given a gold medal and five hundred dollars, which she used to buy a farm. She is considered a hero to this day.[2]

The sinking of the *Rebecca Foster* is a testimony to the ferocity of the lake. As the boat was approaching Long Point from the east, the winds tore the sails to shreds and the helpless vessel was left at the mercy of the waves. So high did the waves roar that they carried the *Rebecca Foster* completely across the sand spit where she finally foundered on the opposite side of Long Point.

There was, however, one sinking that drew the attention of those on shore for an entirely different reason. Because of its proximity to the American shore, rum-running became common during the Prohibition years. In 1922, the *City of Dresden* was en route to "Mexico" (a.k.a. Michigan) with its cargo of Old Crow whisky. Anxious to reach his destination, Captain John McQueen turned his bow into an impending storm. As he approached Long Point, he soon saw that he was in danger of grounding on a sandbar and began to jettison his load. But, as the waves grew higher, the boat began to break up. While the captain and his crew, except one, were rescued by those on shore, those rescuers quickly realized that the cargo was whisky and gathered it up by the bottle, keg, and case, and hustling it into safe storage. By the time the police had arrived, there was none to be seen.

One of the grizzliest sights was that of a lifeboat drifting ashore in a raging blizzard, its entire crew frozen solid by their oars. And, in an eerie premonition, an 1883 blizzard claimed a vessel with a name that a century later, on another ship, would be memorialized in song and in Great Lakes lore. Its name: the *Edmund Fitzgerald*. It didn't help the scenario that a few locals known as "wreckers" would stand on shore holding lanterns to lure the passing ships onto shoals so that they could board and loot them.

It quickly became apparent that safeguards were needed, and, in 1829, following a season of terrible losses, the legislature of Upper Canada commissioned the construction of an eighteen-metre stone lighthouse tower to be built at the tip. But the location quickly proved useless and, in 1843, was replaced with a new twenty-metre-high wooden tower. However, by 1915, the waves and shifting sands were threatening it, too, and in 1916 a third tower of poured concrete, was built, and the wooden tower was burned. The light, which remains standing, was automated in 1989 and still guides vessels safely around the perilous point.

Another lighthouse, which also still stands, seems oddly out of place at first glance. Located seemingly in the middle of a cottage development, it is known as the Old Cut Lighthouse. As early as 1828, a group of locals petitioned for a cut through the isthmus to avoid the dangerous outer point. Approval for a channel 380 metres long was granted in 1833. However, one of the lake's many savage storms saved them trouble. In November 1833, a westerly storm sent a storm surge piling up at the eastern end of the lake. As the wind dropped, the surge reversed direction. Building up as it funnelled through Long Point Bay, it roared across the spit, creating a channel of its own. In 1865, a second storm created an even deeper cut a short distance away. In both cases, the government deepened and stabilized the new channels. And here, in 1879, they erected a thirty-metre-high wooden lighthouse tower with keeper's house attached. However, by 1916, the cut had silted up to the point where ships could no longer traverse it and the light was decommissioned. While the cut has been filled in for roads and cottages, the lighthouse still stands, now used as a residence.

Long Point's "Old Cut" lighthouse may seem out of place, but its location is a result of a fierce storm, which created a cut through the sandy peninsula.

By the 1920s, vacationers had discovered the beaches of Long Point. As the Long Point Club owned only the eastern two-thirds of the spit, the western section, closest to the neck, started to become popular. In 1921, Long Point Provincial Park was created to the west of the Old Cut Lighthouse. But with demand for cottages growing, the province allowed a subdivision of the property, which was then sold for cottages. To accommodate the growing numbers

While the outer reaches of Long Point are off limits, observation decks allow wildlife viewing nearer the shore.

of park users, they opened a new park of 120 (later enlarged to 330 hectares) east of the lighthouse.

Between the park and the neck, cottages and dance halls soon appeared. On the lake side, they were built atop a ridge of sand dunes, and each spring owners can be seen shovelling away the wind-whipped sand from their driveways. In lower sections, many were built on pilings to prevent damage from high waves and storm surges. On the bay side, channels were cut through the marshes to create a Venice-like cottage community. By 1933, inns and dance halls had begun to appear here, as well, with names like the Long Point Lodge, the Old Cut Inn, the Cucumber Inn, and the Highland Dance Hall. To accommodate the growing demand of pleasure boaters and sports fishermen, twelve marinas were cut into the shallow waters of Long Point Bay.

To improve access to the growing community, the government built a crude causeway in 1928 and planted willows to line it. Today, the early bridges are gone and the gravel is roadway now paved, forming part of the highway network.

The most recent evolution of the Point came in 1986 when the United Nations Educational, Scientific, and Cultural Organization (UNESCO) declared the point to a "World Biosphere Reserve." Its unique combination of flora, fauna, and ecosystems has earned it this status. The Long Point Club followed up by donating two-thirds of their own holdings to the Canadian Wildlife Service.

Many of the old cottages are gone, replaced by newer permanent dwellings. Dance halls and inns have given way to convenience stores, restaurants, and boutique summer shops. While the beaches and campgrounds remain popular, the sad irony of Long Point's new status is that, although its wetlands, dunes, and forests form such a distinctive natural feature, and a national treasure, public access to it ends at the park boundary.

Point aux Pins

Although less well-known than many of Ontario's more popular provincial parks, and in the shadow of the nearby Point Pelee National park, Rondeau Provincial Park is Ontario's second oldest, created soon after the establishment of the internationally renowned Algonquin Park in 1893. At first Algonquin was called a "national" park, even though it fell within the provincial purview. The term "national" referred instead to its ecological significance rather than its jurisdiction.

Geographically, Point aux Pins is a "cuspate" sand spit curving eight kilometres into the lake and is one of only two such features in North America. (The other is in Florida.) Before the government cut through the sandbar at the west end of Rondeau Bay, Point aux Pins, in fact, enclosed a lake that French explorers described as the "Ronde Eau." Point aux Pins consists of a series of sand ridges interspersed by linear marshes. The largest of the marshes is designated as a provincially significant wetland.

Of the 3,254 hectares that make up the peninsula, 350 had originally been set aside in 1795 by Lieutenant Governor John Graves Simcoe as a timber reserve for the navy. But it did not lie idle for long. Its first white occupant, around 1809, was reputedly an American trapper named Dickson. His mysterious demise was later attributed to a rival trapper, but the crime was never solved. By 1844, the peninsula was being heavily logged for the harbour improvements then taking place across the bay where the government was cutting through the sandbar.

From 1848 until 1853 Point aux Pins remained the exclusive hunting preserve of a local politician, after which the point became open season for hunters. However, the sandy and infertile soils turned away any settlers, and in 1872, when seventeen lots were surveyed, only one was taken, although fishermen found the bountiful waters full of fish and a substantial fishery developed. Tourists, too, had discovered the beaches and wildlife and began arriving by boat as early as the 1860s from Shrewsbury Landing on the north shore of the bay.

By 1867, the extensive logging was causing concern in the area and local officials complained to the province. To help address their complaints, in 1876, the province appointed a caretaker. But, under his watch, he allowed exploitation to continue and even permitted farmers to let their cattle to roam at will. Then, in 1894, a year after the act was passed creating Algonquin "national" Park, Point aux Pins was designated as a provincial park to be preserved it in "a state of primeval forest," and was given the name Rondeau Provincial Park.

But this "preservation" intent did not happen. The first park superintendent, Isaac Gardiner, felt that the optimal use for the new park was to fully develop it to gain as much revenue as possible. He cleared the forests to expand picnic grounds, added a pavilion, playground, baseball diamond, and a large docking area. To gain even more revenue, he invited the fishermen back and even allowed exploration for gas and oil. He then surveyed forty cottage lots, which were quickly taken up by the merchants of the nearby towns. Hunters, too, were allowed free reign and several hunt clubs built their clubhouses throughout the park. His efforts to lure a hotel failed, however, when the province turned him down, fearing a hotel in a provincial park would unfairly compete with the new hotels at Erieau across the bay. Nature and "forest primeval" were forgotten.

By the late 1970s, practices on the mainland farms brought soils and chemicals pouring into the waters of the bay, causing the aquatic vegetative community to almost disappear. Fish populations followed suit and the fishery collapsed. Now faced with an ecological disaster, the authorities moved to improve conservation practices, restoring the quality of the water.

Today Rondeau is once more a "natural" park, offering opportunities to canoe, camp, and hike along the same roads that Gardiner had built to develop the park. The Carolinian flora is carefully protected, as are the marshes that contain lilies, cattails, and wild rice. Many visitors arrive to view the wildlife and especially the many bird species, such as the tundra swans, which arrive each March. The road that Gardiner built around the circumference of the park is now the South Point Trail and hugs the shoreline while accessing an extensive oak savannah. Point aux Pins and Rondeau Park is at last living up to its original intent.

Some of the park's historic legacy lingers as well. Many of the oldest cottages, as well a yacht club and a pair of churches have been permitted to stay in the park boundary at least until their leases expire in 2017. Although their presence seems at odds with the park's ecological purpose, they also form an important part of the park's historic legacy, a significance not lost on the Heritage Board of Chatham-Kent, which hopes to preserve at least those with architectural merit.

Point Pelee

While Point Pelee's fame centres upon it being mainland Canada's most southerly piece of land, that southern tip doesn't always remain the same. While the forested portion of the point extends eight kilometres from the park's northern boundary, the wave-washed sand spit that curls into the lake may vary between nearly a kilometre from the end of the woodland to nothing. This bare strip of sand earned the point its name, "Pelee," the French term meaning "bald."

As with much of the lake's shoreline, Point Pelee was occupied as much as a thousand years ago by the Neutral Natives. Dollier and Galinée, the two intrepid French missionaries, encountered their misfortune there when, while sleeping, they left much of their gear too close to the water's edge, and when the lake rose up in one of its usual tempests, the waves grabbed much of it, causing them to curtail their planned trip.

Many of the Aboriginal people were still there when government surveyor, Abraham Iradell, surveyed the point in 1799, although by then the Neutrals had been replaced by Iroquois or Wyandotte peoples. Just thirty years earlier, a contingent of troops under Lieutenant Abraham Cuyler, en route to Detroit, had been ambushed by these same occupants, and many were killed or captured. The surveyors also reported back on the valuable timber stands, and the southern 1,550 hectares was established as a naval reserve where the timber could be used to construct British ships.

Despite this designation, squatters were not impressed, and, by the 1830s, several families had illegally moved into the reserve. After the British government turned the reserve over to the Canadian government in 1871, the squatters received title to their land.

For a brief period, as many as twenty-two fishermen operated on the point where their catch was collected by the steamer *Louise* and taken off to Sandusky, Ohio. But pollution and overfishing were common even then and the fishery was short-lived. Longer lasting, however, were the drainage schemes north of the reserve. Here, in what were known as the Mersea Marshes, 1,600 hectares were drained and transformed into arable land, cultivating onions, tomatoes,

The Delaurier squatter's home has been preserved in Point Pelee National Park as a reminder of the point's European settlers.

soybeans, and radishes. In the sandier sections of the reserve, the former squatters and former fishermen raised cattle and hogs, which they allowed to roam freely. Some planted crops such as grapes, asparagus, and peaches, commercial productions that supplied much of southwestern Ontario.

In 1910, the first of the cottages arrived, raising an alarm that a proliferation of buildings would degrade the point's ecosystem. The first to highlight the concern was the National Museum of Canada's chief ornithologist, P.A. Taverner[3], who, in a report to the federal commission of conservation, urged the creation of a national park at Point Pelee. His warnings were heeded and in 1918 an order-in-council created Point Pelee National Park. But the government would wait until 1938 before actually appointing the point's first supervisor. By then, however, authorities realized that the cottages were destroying the natural environment, the very reason that park was established in the first place. The park contained not only the cottages but in the 1930s, two hotels were built as well, the Post Hotel and the Aviation Inn, which was widely praised for its menu.

Since then, the park's operations have moved much more strongly toward protecting the fragile marshes and Carolinian ecosystem. The cottagers are gone, and the last of the hotels closed in 1963. Car traffic, which once was allowed to access the beach, has now been confined to the parking lots. During the peak summer period a shuttle train delivers visitors from the visitor centre to the spit, while during the off-season, cars may drive the route.

The main draw now lies not with the sand beaches as much as it is the flora and fauna that make the park unique in Canada. Among the Carolinian plants are others like the prickly-pear cactus. The park protects more than seven hundred species of plants in ecological zones such dry forests, grasslands, and cedar savannahs. The forest cover ranges from dense jungle-like vine-covered trees to open grasslands. Much of the park consists of marshland with the usual cattails and bulrushes, lily pads, and the hop tree, a species found as far south as Mexico. While the bears and deer, once common in the forests, have long vanished, other species such as bats, frogs, turtles, and snakes are commonplace. In 1994, the tiny southern flying squirrel was reintroduced.

A modern interpretation centre allows visitors to appreciate this natural treasure trove. From the centre a variety of trails make their way through the varying ecosystems. And, to recall the human heritage of the point, the De Laurier squatter's homestead, built in the 1830s, has been preserved as a museum piece and is a testimony to the earliest settlement of the point.

Heritage plaques along the trails also recount the fishery and the life-saving station, all of which have long vanished.

The most-awaited season in the park, however, occurs during September when the migrating monarch butterflies turn the trees and bushes into a quivering fantasyland of orange and yellow. This colourful spectacle attracts thousands of nature lovers to the park for the butterflies' brief layover.

The problem of the disappearing sand spit is not entirely nature's doing. The many new marinas and erosion-control groins along the shore between the point and Colchester Harbour are capturing the moving sands and preventing them from being carried to the point where storm waves wash away the sand now with little or no replenishment. Ironically, those very protection devices cause the offshore waters to deepen and threaten the shoreline owners with larger and more destructive waves.

Pelee Island

While Pelee Island does not form a point of land as such, it shares much of the appearance and the legacy of those that do. When the ice sheets of the last great ice age began to recede, the lake level was lower and Pelee Island formed part of a land bridge, along with the many other islands that congregated at the western end of the lake. Archaeologists have discovered that Aboriginal peoples inhabited Pelee as far back as 10,000 years ago, when the island may well have been a point of the mainland. The early travellers described it as the "Island of Point au Pelee."

European interest in Pelee began in 1788 when an agent named Thomas McKee concluded an agreement with the resident population of Ojibway and Ottawa Indians, whereby in return for an annual donation of three bushels of corn, McKee could have the island for 999 years. Just what he had in mind is not known, although with a Loyalist wave beginning to sweep Upper Canada, speculation might have been a possibility. But more likely it was the island's plentiful timber supply. The dense stands of red cedar were in high demand, and, as early as 1797, McKee was shipping off timber to Amherstburg for the construction of Fort Amherstburg.

The lease then passed to McKee's son, Alexander, who in turn leased it to John Askin. Askin brought the first white settlers to island, logging men who were interested in not just the cedar but the white oak for shipbuilding. But the one individual who was most responsible for developing Pelee Island was William McCormick. In 1815, he purchased the lease and set about quarrying the island's valuable limestone that lay at the surface, providing material for buildings as far away as Christ Church in Colchester, west of Kingsville, and for the island's own lighthouse, as well. McCormick, whose career included shopkeeper and postmaster at Colchester, member of the Legislative Assembly, and magistrate, is regarded as the founder of settlement on Pelee Island.

But the island was not to be left in peace, at least not yet. In 1838, the Upper Canada Rebellion was in full swing and had garnered support from "patriots" living in the United States. In February of that year, a group of rebels made their way across the ice of the lake set on "capturing" Pelee Island. Alerted to the invasion, troops of the 32nd Militia and 83rd Regiment set out from Fort Malden. They quickly reached the island and, in a pre-dawn attack, surprised the rebels on the south end of the island. After a brief battle, the outnumbered rebels stumbled their way back across the lake. And so was fought what has become known as the "battle of Pelee Island."

But settlement remained light. In 1846, W.H. Smith said of "Point Pele Island": "it has never been surveyed; consequently, the number of acres it

Ontario Archives, Acc 9141, S 13352.

An early steamship on its way to Pelee Island.

contains is not known. About half the island is fit for cultivation. Contains about fifty inhabitants. The island is well supplied with red cedar and possesses a fine limestone quarry. There is a grist mill on the island and a light house on the north east point." Two docks had been built and steamers called occasionally to ship out the timber and the quarry stones.

As late as 1854, the title to the island remained in dispute. Appealing an earlier government decision that McCormick had never obtained rightful title to the island, his descendents succeeded in reversing that decision and the land was surveyed into eleven plots of 120 hectares for each of McCormick's heirs. In 1866, the government was able to begin issuing title to other parts of the island, as well.

It was then that Captain David McCormick, William's grandson, brought a winemaker from Kentucky, D.J. Williams, to the island where, along with David's brother Thomas, and Thaddeus Smith, they began Ontario's first winemaking operation. By 1868, one of the island's most important heritage structures, the Vin Villa wine cellar, was finished. The wine cellar went down four metres into solid bedrock, while the stone house above contained eight gables and a pillared porch. Winemaking quickly caught on. In 1890, the Pelee Island Wine and Vineyard Company had added a large wine cellar and Pelee Island wine was being marketed around the world. But the era would not last. By 1898, wine faced an international financial crisis and many of the island's vineyards switched to tobacco-growing.

But most of the island remained marshy lowland, much of it below lake level. Indeed, one portion of higher ground even went by the name "Middle Island." Because no roads had yet penetrated the marshes, the islanders were connected to each other only by a series of eight docks built all around the island. As early as 1878, the potential of the marshland for crops was recognized — if they could be drained and kept above the water level. In 1885, two Ohio businessmen, Lemuel Brown of Cleveland and Dr. John Scudder of Cincinnati, bought 1,600 hectares of marsh and put steam dredges to work draining them. Within five years, eighteen kilometres of canals had been cleared, while pumps kept the marshland above the water level. When tobacco-growing shifted to the sands of Norfolk County in the 1920s, the farmers on Pelee replaced the crop with soy beans and seed corn. In 1935, to handle the shipping, a grain elevator was built at the Scudder dock on the island's north end.

At the time of Pelee Island's first winemaking period, tourists began to take interest in the cool breezes and uncrowded ambience of the island. One

The lodge that forms the focus for the Pelee Island Club has survived for more than a century.

of the first tourist hotels was the Breeze Place Hotel, while the Vin Villa took in tourists, as well. Much of the attraction was the bountiful fishing, and in 1883, the Pelee Club was formed by wealthy American businessmen. Located on sixteen hectares of land at the northwest corner of the island, the club consisted of a main building with forty rooms, as well as a bowing alley, billiard room, and boathouses all lit with gas and supplied with running water. Among the club's members over the years were American general Philip Sheridan, railcar builder George Pullman, and American presidents Grover Cleveland, Rutherford Hayes, and Howard Taft. Although the bowling alley is used only for storage, the original lodge still stands and the membership remains exclusive. These days, however, instead of fishing, the attraction is the annual pheasant hunt.

Commercial fishing took place at Fish Point, the island's southernmost point. In 1900, open boats would haul in herring, pike, whitefish, and pickerel for sale to fish buyers, Post and Company, from Sandusky, Ohio. The buyers in later years became the Omstead Fishery of Wheatley.

The Jiimaan *car ferry provides daily service from Leamington or Kingsville to Pelee Island.*

While the landscape of Pelee Island is continuously changing with the building of more homes, it can still boast of a substantial historic legacy. Sadly, the elegant Vin Villa burned in 1963, and its historic ruins are off limits to the public. Today, the shrub-infested stone shell can only be discerned through a wrought-iron fence. The Scudder grain elevator was taken down in the year 2000, but the dock has been landscaped and now harbours pleasure craft. And here, while a newer co-op store supplies the grocery needs of the north end, the historic McCormick store is being renovated as a dwelling.

The north end of the island can boast of Pelee's oldest buildings, including a limestone home, and a log storage shed that was once an early dwelling, possibly the island's first. The historic 1833 lighthouse has been restored, although because of high water, access is sometimes difficult.

Today, the island's key point of entry has shifted from Scudder to the West Dock where a small village includes a motel, restaurants, and the Pelee Island Heritage Centre, a museum housed in the 1911 former town hall. Here, too, at an enlarged wharf, the *Pelee Islander,* the means of transportation since 1966 and the newer car ferry, the *Jiimaan*, bring tourists and residents from Leamington and Kingsville on the Canadian side and from Sandusky, Ohio, on the American side.

Anyone who has walked into a liquor store in Ontario will know that Pelee Island is once again famous for its wines. Just a short walk from the West Dock pier, where the ferries dock, the landscaped winery offers a patio, a snack bar, and an historic display of photos and winemaking equipment. While newer homes and bed and breakfast accommodation can be found around the island, the largest concentration of summer homes lines the sandy eastern beaches. However, storm surges, which are at their worst under an east wind, have prompted most homeowners to erect their dwellings on stilts.

Despite its southerly latitude, Pelee Island is not Canada's most southerly point of land. That distinction belongs to Middle Island, which lies just off Fish Point and only one hundred metres from the United States border. That is likely why its lasting notoriety is that of supplying illicit liquor to the Americans during Prohibition, much of which went to the infamous Purple Gang of Detroit, although Chicago gangster Al Capone was also alleged to have visited the island. Joseph Boscoe's hotel and gaming house was considered to be the base of operations for the rum-running. An airstrip, built before 1950, now lies beneath a cover of vegetation. Today, Boscoe's hotel is a ruin and the island, now a protected part of the Point Pelee National Park, is off limits to visitors, especially rum-runners.

NOTES

Chapter 1

1. Michael C. Hanson, *The History of Lake Erie*, Columbus Ohio, the Ohio Geological Survey, Ohio Department of Natural Resources, December 1999.

2. Much of the hydrogeology of Lake Erie is summarized in the *Canadian Encyclopaedia* under "Lake Erie."

3. The sighting was reported in the *Buffalo Express* newspaper in July 1873 (no specific date has been recorded). The paper quoted one of the observers as saying: "It must have been part whale because it would spout water from its nostrils as high as twenty feet above his head." A later edition of the paper stated in an editorial that the monster sightings were results of alcohol or hoaxes. Further information can be found at http://www.pararesearchers.org and "Lake Erie Monster?" by Graham Marsden, http://www.fishingmagic.com (accessed January 31, 2009).

Chapter 2

1. Information on the early Lake Erie tribes is comprehensively covered at http://www.accessgeneology.com under the "Index of Tribes." http://www.accessgenealogy.com (accessed January 31, 2009).

2. The Jesuit Missionaries operated a string of missions among the Huron

people, including missions at St. Louis and St. Joseph, as well as Ste. Marie near modern-day Midland. Although excavations of the Ste. Marie site date back to 1855, it was the work of the late Wilfred Jury that brought to light the nature of the mission. When restoration, which began in 1964, was complete and opened to the public, it was named Ste. Marie Among the Hurons. (Source: *The Canadian Encyclopedia.*)

3. Wilfred Jury is a respected archaeologist. He founded the Museum of Indian Archaeology and Pioneer Life in 1933 as part of the University of Western Ontario. As both an amateur and professional archaeologist, Jury collected artifacts from numerous sites throughout southwestern Ontario. In the late 1920s, his collection had grown to over 6,000 artifacts. Jury also conducted many archaeological investigations, including the Iona Earthworks, and the site of the Willow Creek depot near Barrie, Ontario.

4. At age twenty-three, Louis Jolliet decided to become a *coureur de bois.* In 1668, he outfitted himself out with trade goods from the merchant Charles Aubert de la Chesnaye: "two guns, two pistols, six packets of *rassades* [glass beads], twenty-four axes, a gross of small bells, twelve ells of Iroquois-style cloth, ten ells of linens, forty pounds of tobacco ..." However, he actually bought the goods for his brother, Adrien Jolliet, who left with them. Hence, Adrien is the "Jolliet" whom we hear of as being in the Great Lakes area during the ensuing months. (Source: *Canadian Museum of Civilization.*)

5. René de Bréhant de Galinée (1645–1678) was a member of the order of St. Sulpice at Montreal, although he trained as a mathematician and mapmaker. Like the Jesuits, the Sulpicians wanted to extend their missionary work among the western Native tribes. François Dollier de Casson (1636–1701) was also a Sulpician missionary, becoming the Sulpician Superior in Montreal.

In 1669, the two embarked on a dangerous journey through a little-known region to reach the western tribes. Both men kept diaries of the trip. Galinée's manuscript was found in 1847 by Pierre Margry, who copied it, giving the transcripts to Francis Parkman and several Canadian historians. In 1875, the Historical Society of Montreal published a version of it that was later translated into English by James H. Coyne, and published in Volume 4 of the Ontario Historical Society's *Papers and Records*, 1904. The original manuscript is in the Bibliothèque Nationale in Paris. De Casson's account of the journey was lost. The quotes are from Galinée's diary.

Chapter 3

1. Born at Castle Malahide in the County of Dublin in 1771, Thomas Talbot joined Upper Canada's lieutenant governor, John Graves Simcoe, in 1793 as his personal secretary. Simcoe asked the English government to grant Talbot 2,000 hectares along the Lake Erie shore on which to encourage settlers. For every settler he put onto a twenty-hectare parcel, Talbot himself would receive sixty hectares, up to a maximum of 2,000 hectares, although his total holdings ended up being more extensive than that. After returning to England for a stint in the military, Talbot returned to Lake Erie in 1803 and established his base at Port Talbot. By 1836, he had succeeded in settling significant portions of twenty-nine townships along the Erie shore, an area which by then had 30,000 residents. To qualify for possession, Talbot insisted that the applicant actually clear the land and establish a home on it. (Source: *The Canadian Encyclopaedia.*)

2. The Erie Canal: First proposed in 1808, the Erie Canal was constructed between 1817 and 1825 and provided the first transportation route between the eastern seaboard and the western interior of the United States, replacing the slower land transport by draft animals. It also cut transportation costs by about 95 percent. The canal opened up western New York State and regions farther west to settlement, and made New York City a major port. It was expanded between 1834 and 1862. In 1918, the original canal was replaced by the larger New York State Barge Canal. Today it is mainly used by recreational watercraft.

3. Opened in 1835, the Grand River Canal linked Brantford with Lake Erie. The brainchild of David Thompson, the canal consisted of six locks, as well as a turning basin in Brantford. The canal allowed the transport of gypsum, lumber, and farm products to the port of Dunnville on small barges, where the material was trans-shipped onto large lake vessels. The

canal fell into disuse through the 1870s as rail lines were built into the area. It was officially closed in 1895.

Chapter 4

1. Fenians were members of a movement initiated in 1857 by Irish-Americans to secure Irish independence from Britain. Between 1866 and 1871 they attempted a series of incursions into Canada, including an attack on Ridgeway, where they defeated the local militia before retiring. During this foray they briefly occupied the ruins of Fort Erie.

2. The Niagara Movement began in Fort Erie in 1905 when its delegates were unable to obtain accommodations in Buffalo. It was in Fort Erie that the movement's founder, W.E.B. Dubois, a black intellectual, and delegates from thirteen states and District of Columbia, laid the groundwork for the National Association for the Advancement of Coloured People. No delegates from Canada were invited, and its journal, the *Crisis*, was essentially ignored Canada. (Source: R.W. Winks, *The Blacks in Canada*.)

3. Arriving in Canada from Russia in 1842, Casimir Gzowski (later knighted), trained as an engineer and became superintendent of public works in the Province of Canada. As chief engineer for the Grand Trunk Railway between 1852 and 1850, he constructed the Grand Trunk Railway from Montreal to Sarnia. When a railway bridge was needed over the Niagara, he was given the assignment. He later served as aide-de-camp to Queen Victoria.

4. In 1893, Alonzo Mather proposed a multi-purpose bridge between Fort Erie and Buffalo, which would be able to carry steam trains, trolleys, carriages, wagons, and pedestrians. It would be financially supported by revenue from an electric-generating project Mather was proposing for the location, as well. The plans, however, were thwarted by electric-generating interest on the American side. In 1919, William Eckert then re-activated Mather's scheme, dropping the railway component, and focusing on the growing motor vehicle traffic. His plans were approved in 1925 by the International Joint Commission, and the bridge opened on June 1, 1927.

5. This quote is from the *Illustrated Historical Atlas of the Counties of Essex and Kent*, published by H. Belden and Company, Toronto, 1880.

Chapter 5

1. In 1912, Quebec-born Mack Sennett moved to California where he founded Keystone Studios. Here he perfected the slapstick comedy with their car chases and pie-throwing. Many of his films included a bevy of swimsuit-clad young ladies known as the "Sennett Bathing Beauties." This early titillation proved popular in the movie houses, many of which were found in the growing numbers of amusement parks across North America.

2. The Chautauqua movement began in the late nineteenth century as an adult education movement in Upper New York State on the shores of Chautauqua Lake and became highly popular. Chautauqua assemblies expanded and spread throughout North America, bringing speakers, teachers, musicians, entertainers, preachers, and specialists of the day. The movement faded during the 1920s with the popularity of moving pictures.

3. Much information on the dance pavilions at Erie Beach, Crystal Beach, and other amusement parks such as those at Port Stanley, Rondeau, and Bob-Lo Island are recounted in Peter Yong's book, *Let's Dance: A Celebration of Ontario's Dance Halls and Summer Dance Pavilions* (Toronto: Natural Heritage/ Natural History Inc., 2003).

Chapter 6

1. The Grand River Treaty. In 1784, the Six Nations of the Mohawk Valley designated the Tyendenaga chief, Joseph Brant, to discuss with Sir Frederick Haldimand their fears of persecution at the hands of the Americans for their role in having aided the British during the American Revolution. On January 14, 1793, Lieutenant John Simcoe confirmed by patent under the Great Seal, a grant of land to the Six Nations, one which extended ten kilometres back from each bank of the river from its mouth to its source, a grant which covered about 276,000 hectares. Most of that, however, had

been surrendered to the Crown by 1846 to allow settlers to take up land for farming.

Chapter 7

1. Smith's quotes on Port Rowan are found in the *Illustrated Historical Atlas of the County of Norfolk*, published by H.R. Page (Toronto) in 1877.

2. The Père Marquette Railroad was incorporated in 1900 in Michigan, an amalgam of three existing lines. In 1892, the Grand Trunk had walked away from its lease with the London and Port Stanley Railway, which was later leased to the Père Marquette Railway. But that, too, lapsed and, in 1913, the City of London took over the lease and rebuilt the line, electrifying it in the process. In 1947, the Père Marquette merged with the Chesapeake and Ohio Railway, and is now known as CSX. (Source: *The Ontario Railway History Page*, http://home.primus.ca/~robkath/.)

Chapter 8

1. Following the Rebellion of 1837, John George Lambton, Earl of Durham, was appointed to investigate the grievances of the supporters of the rebellion. In what is called the "Durham Report," his two main recommendations were the union of the two Canadas and a move to more responsible government, one in which the government executive would come from the majority party in power, and no longer from an exclusive "Family Compact." While his recommendations for a union were rejected out of hand by the French of Lower Canada, responsible government came into play in 1847. This brought about not just a party system, but more responsibilities for local government and the emergence of a more extensive system of county level governments.

Chapter 9

1. The description of Port Royal is found in the *Illustrated Historical of the County of Norfolk* (Toronto: H.R. Belden, 1877).

2. During Talbot's reign, a number of roads were surveyed through the

region that used the name "Talbot." Although the original Talbot Road ran from Brantford to Delhi, funds ran out before it could go farther. In 1809, Mahlon Burwell, deputy surveyor for Upper Canada, extended the road from Delhi to Port Talbot. In 1811, Burwell laid out Talbot Road West from a village near St. Thomas, named Talbotville, to Sandwich, today's Windsor. Two other "Talbot Roads" lead from Westminister, near London, to St. Thomas, and from Ridgetown to Windsor. A tourist route known today as the "Talbot Trail" follows the former Provincial Highway 3 and in only a few places traces any of the original "Talbot Roads."

3.   On page 145 of his book, *Blacks in Canada*, Winks describes the conditions of the black settlements in Amherstburg, Sandwich, and Colchester in Essex County, where they suffered discrimination and violent attacks. The settlement at Colchester was in particular not well regarded.

Chapter 10

1.   The late Joseph W. Csubak was a long-time member of the Long Point Conservation Authority Board of Directors, serving from 1980 to 1998. An ardent naturalist, he led the initiative to clear an area at the top of the Turkey Point bluff in order to allow visitors a view of the valuable marshlands below. (Source: Janice Robertson, supervisor of Community Relations, Long Point Region Conservation Authority.)

2.   Known as the "Heroine of Long Point," Abigail Becker was a settler on the shore of Long Point, and was used to the storms that sent many a vessel onto the ever-shifting sandbars around the point. During such a tempest on November 24, 1854, a schooner, the *Conductor,* was washed onto a nearby sandbar. The captain and crew, most from Buffalo, managed to stay with the vessel until dawn when Abigail found the men clinging precariously to the rigging. Although she could not swim, she waded into the waves and urged the men to swim for shore. The captain and six crew members, although frozen, made it to shore that morning, a seventh crew member was not rescued until the next day. For her heroics, she received $350 from the sailors and merchants of Buffalo, as well as gold medal struck by the New York Lifesaving Benevolent Association. In addition she received a handwritten letter and £50 from Queen Victoria; a letter of

praise from Governor General Lord Aberdeen; and a bronze medal from the Royal Humane Society. (Source: *The Canadian Encyclopedia.*)

3. Percy A. Taverner was appointed to the National Museum of Canada in 1911 as the museum's ornithologist. He played an important role in wildlife conservation, such as the designation of Point Pelee as a national park, as well as protecting Bonaventure Island and Perce Rock in Quebec. He authored several books including the authoritative *Birds of Canada*, published in 1934. (Source: J.L. Cranmer-Byng, in *The Canadian Encyclopedia.*)

BIBLIOGRAPHY

Amherstburg Bicentennial Book Committee. *Amherstburg, 1796–1996: The New Town on the Garrison Grounds,* 2 Vols. Amherstburg, ON: 1997.

Ashdown, Dana. *Railway Steamships of Ontario.* Erin, ON: Boston Mills Press, 1988.

Barrett, Harry B. *Lore and Legends of Long Point.* Don Mills ON: Burns and MacEachern, 1977.

Boyle, Terry, *Memories of Ontario: A Traveller's Guide to the Towns and Cities of Western Ontario.* Toronto: Cannonbooks, 1991.

Burns, Noel M. *Erie: The Lake That Survived.* Totawa, NJ: Rowman and Allanheld Publishers, 1985.

Canadian Encyclopedia, The. Year 2000 Edition, Toronto: McClelland and Stewart, 1999.

Chapman, L.J. and D.F. Putnam. *Physiography of Southern Ontario.* Toronto: University of Toronto Press, 1966.

Colombo, John Robert. *Mysteries of Ontario,* Toronto: Hounslow Press/The Dundurn Group, 1999.

Conway, Ruby. *Tales of Tennessee*. Port Colborne, ON: M.V. Lohnes, 1994.

Cooper, Charles. *Hamilton's Other Railway*. Ottawa: Bytown Railway Society, 2001.

Cowan, E.R. and J. Paine. *The Introduction of Individual Transferable Quotas to the Lake Erie Fishery*. Ottawa: Fisheries and Oceans Canada, 1997.

Dollier de Casson, François, and René de Bréhant de Galinée. *Exploration of the Great Lakes, 1669–1670*. Translated and edited by James H. Coyne. Toronto: Ontario Historical Society, 1903.

Eldridge Richard. *Dunnville: An Historical Walking Tour*. Dunnville, ON: Dunnville Chamber of Commerce, 1991.

Fort Erie Museum Board. *Many Voices: A Collective History of Greater Fort Erie*, 1996.

Fraser, Chad. *Lake Erie Stories*. Toronto: Dundurn Press, 2008.

Galinée, René de Bréhant. *Exploration of the Great Lakes, 1669–1670*. Translated by James H. Coyne, Toronto: Ontario Historical Society, 1903.

Gervais, C.H. *The Rumrunners: A Prohibition Primer*. Scarborough, ON: Firefly Books, 1984.

Gorrie, Peter. "Ecological Treasure of Lake Erie Under Assault." *Canadian Geographic*, Vol. 115, No. 3 (May/June 1995): 81.

Grady, Wayne, *The Great Lakes: The Natural History of a Changing Region*. Toronto: Greystone Books, 2007.

Graham, J. Robertson. *Where Canada Begins: A Visitor's Guide to Point Pelee National Park*. n.p., n.d.

Grainger, Jennifer. *Vanished Villages of Elgin*. Toronto: Dundurn Press, 2008.

Hanson, Michael C. *The History of Lake Erie*. Columbus, OH: The Ohio Geological Survey, Ohio Department of Natural Resources, December 1999.

Hazen, Sharon, ed. *Down by the Bay; A History of Long Point and Port Rowan, 1799–1999*. Erin, ON: Boston Mills Press, 2000.

Hepburn, Agnes M. *Historical Sketch of the Village of Port Stanley*. Port Stanley, ON: Port Stanley Women's Institute, 1952.

Hooper, Marion McCormick. *Pelee Island Then and Now*. Author, 1967.

Illustrated Historical Atlas of the County of Elgin. Toronto: H.R. Page & Co., 1877.

Illustrated Historical Atlas of the Counties of Essex and Kent. Toronto: H. Belden and Co., 1880–1881.

Illustrated Historical Atlas of the Counties of Lincoln and Welland. Toronto: H.R. Page & Co., 1876.

Illustrated Historical Atlas of the County of Norfolk. Toronto: H.R. Page & Co., 1877.

Imlach, W.I. *An Old Man's Memories*. Reprinted from the *Dunnville Chronicle*, 1900.

Jackson, John N., and J. Burtniak. *Railways in the Niagara Peninsula*. Belleville, ON: Mika Publishers, 1978.

Jackson, Matt. "Dangerous Waters: Lake Erie's Mysterious Deadly Quadrangle." *The Beaver*, Vol. 84, No. 3 (June /July 2004): 36–39.

Jameson, Anna. *Winter Studies and Summer Rambles in Canada*. Toronto: McClelland and Stewart, Toronto, 1990.

Killan, Gerald. *Protected Places: A History of Ontario's Provincial Park System*. Toronto: Queen's Printer, 1993.

Lauriston, Victor. *Romantic Kent: More Than Three Centuries of History, 1626–1952*. Author, 1952.

Leader, Mrs. R.W. *Wheatley Village*. Author, 1951.

Leamington District Chamber of Commerce. *Leamington, A Walk Through History*. n.d.

McCullough, A.B. *The Commercial Fishery of the Canadian Great Lakes*. Ottawa: Ministry of the Environment, 1989.

MacDonald, Cheryl Emily. *Grand Heritage: A History of Dunnville (and the Surrounding Townships)*. Dunnville, ON: Dunnville District Heritage Association, 1992.

MacDonald, Cheryl Emily. *Heritage Highlights: Stories From Haldimand and Norfolk*. Simcoe, ON: Heritage Writing Services, 1994.

MacDonald, Cheryl Emily, *Norfolk Folk, Immigration and Migration in Norfolk County*. Simcoe, ON: Norfolk Folk Book Committee, 1995.

Marsh, John A. *With the Tide, Recollections of the Town of Amherstburg*. Amherstburg, ON: Marsh Collection Society, 1995.

Milner, Bruce. *Lakelore: A History of the Fishing Industry Along the North Shore of Lake Erie*. Simcoe, ON: Norfolk School of Agriculture, 1973.

Morris, Stan. *The Front Page: 100 Years of Port Dover News*. Port Dover, ON: Author, 1979.

Mutrie, R. Robert. *The Long Point Settlers*. Ridgeway, ON: Log Cabin Publishing, 1992.

Newland, Laura. *A History of Leamington*. Typed manuscript, in the Leamington Public Library, 1947.

Niagara Parks Commission. *Old Fort Erie: A War of 1812 Garrison*, n.d.

Parks Canada. *Fort Malden: A Walking Tour*, n.d.

Pelee Island. Published by the Township of Pelee Island, n.d.

Port Ryerse Historial and Environnemental Association. *Port Ryerse, 1774–1994*. Port Ryerse, ON, 1994.

Prothero, Frank. *Memories: A History of Port Burwell*. Port Stanley, ON: Nan-Sea Publications, 1986.

Prothero, Frank. *The Good Years; A History of the Commercial Fishing Industry on Lake Erie*. Belleville, ON: Mika Publishing, 1973.

Prothero, Frank and Nancy. *Tales From the North Shore*. Port Stanley, ON: Nan-Sea Publications, 1987.

Rayburn, Alan. *Place Names of Ontario*. Toronto: University of Toronto Press, 1997.

Raymond, Marguerite. *Tales of the Old Town: A History of Fort Erie*. Fort Erie: Fort Erie Historical Museum, 1990.

Rhodes, John. *Rails to the Heartland: A Pictorial History of Kent's Railways*. Chatham, ON: Author, 1991.

Rossi, Erno. *Crystal Beach: The Good Old Days*. Port Colborne, ON: Seventy-Seven Publishers, 2005.

Sims, Hugh Joffrey. *Sims' History of Elgin County*. St. Thomas, ON: Elgin County Library, 1984.

Smith, William H. *Smith's Canadian Gazeteer*. Toronto: H. and W. Rowsell, 1846.

Snell, Frances, S. *Leamington's Heritage, 1874–1974*. Town of Leamington, 1974.

Sobol, Julie MacFie. *Lake Erie: A Pictorial History*. Erin, ON: Boston Mills Press, 2004.

Sobol, Ken. *Looking For Lake Erie: Travels Around a Great Lake*. Toronto: Viking Press, 1995.

Spear, A.W. *The Peace Bridge, 1927–1977, and Reflections of the Past*. Buffalo, NY: The Buffalo and Fort Erie Bridge Company, 1977.

Stewart, Walter and Wolf Kutnahorsky. "The Ills of Lake Erie." *Canadian Geographic*, Vol. 123, No. 5 (Sept/Oct 2003): 36–46.

Tiessen, Ronald. *A Bicycle Guide to Pelee Island*. Pelee Island Heritage Centre, 1992.

Tobzun, Rita. *Wheatley's Story*. n.p., 1982.

Wallace, Madeline. *Memories of Lake Erie Shores*. Essex, ON: Kerch Publications 1984.

Watson, O.K. "Early History of Shrewsbury." In *Kent Historical Society, Papers and Addresses*, Vol. 6 (1924): 82–84.

Winks, Robin W. *The Blacks in Canada: A History*. Montreal: McGill-Queen's University Press, 1971.

Wright, Larry and Patricia. *Great Lakes Lighthouses Encyclopedia*. Erin, ON: Boston Mills Press, 2006.

Young, Peter. *Let's Dance: A Celebration of Ontario's Dance Halls and Summer Dance Pavilions*. Toronto: Natural Heritage/Natural History, Inc., 2002.

WEBSITES

"Bois Blanc Island History." http://www.inselhausbandb.com/history.

"Bob-Lo Island, Detroit River Amusement Park."
    http://www.boblosteamers.com/island.html.

"Closed Canadian Parks." http://cec.chebucto.org/ClosPark/CCPIndex.html.

"Lake Erie Fast Ferry Proposal." http://www.norfolkcounty.ca.

"Lake Erie Monster?" http://www.fishingmagic.com.
    See also http://www.parareasearchers.org for information on "Bessie."

"Ontario's Lake Monsters." http://www.pararesearchers.org.

"Port Colborne residents sue INCO."
    http://www.cbc.ca/canada/story/2001/03/27/inco_lawsuit010327.html.

"Port Colborne Studies," Ontario Ministry of Energy. http://www.ene.gov.on.ca.

"Sand Hill Park History." http://www.sandhillpark.com.

"Wainfleet Bog," Niagara Region Conservation Authority.
    http://www.conservation-niagara.on.ca.

All above websites were accessed between May and September 2008.

INDEX

ABOUT THE AUTHOR

RON BROWN has published many books, including *Back Roads of Ontario, Toronto's Lost Villages, Ontario's Ghost Town Heritage,* and *The Train Doesn't Stop Here Anymore.* He is a member of the Travel Media Association of Canada and chaired the Writers' Union of Canada. He lives in Toronto.

Also by Ron Brown

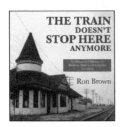

The Train Doesn't Stop Here Anymore

978-1-55002-794-5

$29.99

At one time, railways were the country's economic lifeline, and the station our social centre. Across Canada, stations have been bulldozed and rails ripped up. Once the heart of communities, stations and tracks have left little more than gaping holes in the landscape. This book celebrates the survival of our railway heritage in stations that have been saved or remain in use.

Of Related Interest

Lake Erie Stories
Struggle and Survival on a Freshwater Ocean
By Chad Fraser

978-1-55002-782-2

$24.99

Lake Erie has been the stage for some of the most dramatic events to occur on this continent. This fascinating book, based on thorough research, extensive travels, and first-hand accounts, explores the remarkable personalities and harrowing events that have shaped the lake and the towns and cities that surround it.